CHOOSING HEAVEN

UNDERSTANDING WHAT THE BIBLE TEACHES ABOUT ETERNAL LIFE

CHOOSING HEAVEN

UNDERSTANDING WHAT THE BIBLE TEACHES ABOUT ETERNAL LIFE

BY: FRED HENNES

DEDICATION

My dedication of this book goes to my wife Maredith - my faithful partner in life and ministry. I also would like to express my appreciation to the people of GateWay Bible Church who have provided the environment for me to develop the hands and heart of a pastor. Many thanks to Terri Buller, Rachael Yanez, Floyd Kvamme, Jo Romaniello, Connie Fransen, and Joyce Timm for the help they provided in editing this book. Finally, I'm indebted to three men who have impacted me greatly in my faith: Alan Roberts, Steve Clifford and Ron Marsh.

ABOUT THIS BOOK

This book is written for those who desire clarity regarding their life after death and are open to consider what the Bible teaches about this subject. Since death is the common experience of humankind, we should to be prepared for its arrival. The finality of death on Earth will usher us into the birth of our eternity beyond. The quality of our eternal life will be determined by the decisions we make in this life. This book is a guide to help every person make wise decisions today, before tomorrow catches up with us.

Choosing Heaven attempts to clearly, yet simply, reveal what the Bible teaches regarding death, Heaven and attaining eternal life. This book is based on the authors research and understanding of the Bible which includes over one hundred references to various books and statements found in the Holy Scriptures. The most common views of life after death are contrasted with a simplified view of Heaven gleaned from the Bible. It is a highly recommended read for everyone facing their own mortality.

ABOUT THE AUTHOR

Fred spent 17 years in the world of high-tech manufacturing and the last 27 years as a pastor. He holds a master's degree in Biblical Studies from Trinity Theological Seminary. Fred has been on staff at two churches. The first was at Santa Cruz Bible Church as the Executive Pastor working closely with Pastor Chip Ingram. The second is GateWay Bible Church in Scotts Valley, California where he serves as the Senior Pastor. Fred has been married to Maredith since 1980. They have three married children: Valerie (Dan), Jeffrey (Shauna), and Nate (Bekah). God has blessed them with four young grandchildren: Audrey, Avery, Ryker and Shyla. Fred's greatest passion in life is to know Christ and to make Him known. He rejoices in seeing lives change through the power of God's grace and truth. His hobbies include biking, basketball, ocean fishing, cooking, gardening and reading.

TABLE OF CONTENTS

x

READmTHIS FIRST

"Man's chief end is to glorify God, and to enjoy him forever."

Westminster Shorter Catechism

I am no stranger to death. Five members of my family have died, including one of my brothers (a best friend to me). As a pastor, I have officiated at nearly one hundred funerals, memorial services or graveside burials. I have been with people on the day of their death and during the hour of their death. I have ministered to parents who have lost children and children who have lost parents. I have looked into the eyes of those longing for the assurance that their loved one is now with God in Heaven.

I have witnessed the pain and sorrow caused by the separation of death. Gathered with families in grief, I have observed a universal belief, regardless of religious background, that the one they love lives on in a place with no more suffering and no more tears. This belief is sometimes no more than wishful thinking. There appears to be no basis for this belief other than the deceased was a "good person."

I've wondered if our eternity merely rests on being a good person, and if so, then how good does one need to be to be deemed good enough? Is there anyone terrible enough to be barred from Heaven, and if so, how bad does one need to be to be considered not good enough?

Death is a fascinating subject. I have heard it said that life is one long series of good-byes. Relative to everything in life that will happen to us, nothing is more definitive or final than death.

As significant as it will be for every one of us, death is minimally discussed, planned for, or anticipated. Nothing has a more substantial impact on our present experience than our vision and expectation of the future. A woman who joyfully discovers that she is pregnant feels entirely different on the day she is heading into labor. The undergraduate student arriving on campus the first day of classes feels much different than the graduate leaving college. We are wise to ponder our fate and prepare to enter it confidently.

Outside of the diagnosis of a terminal disease or the departure of someone close to us, death is a subject often avoided. Though death is inevitable, we have become very good at denying its reality, ignoring its eventuality, and dismissing its permanence. All too many are satisfied with unsubstantiated fantasies viewing death as "being in a better place." For the majority, the cultural norm and hope is that the deceased simply "rest-in-peace."

Significantly, I have come alongside many people who view death, and life beyond, through the teachings of the Christian faith. Often, such people do not fear death as many do, for they have confidence about their eternal destiny. I have been refreshed by those who possess peace and assurance that they will meet up again with deceased loved ones. Fortunately for all of us, "God has set eternity in the human heart;" (Ecclesiastes 3:11). and He has given us the insight to attain, and know with complete certainty, where our destiny lies. We are wise to ponder our fate and prepare to enter it confidently.

This book attempts to clearly reveal what the Bible teaches regarding death and the possession of eternal life. My writing is based on my own research and understanding of the Bible, complete with dozens of references to various books and statements in the Bible. In several cases, where the Bible does not make a definitive statement about a topic such as: "Do pets go to heaven?" I have looked at the relevant text associated with the subject and have drawn a reasonable, though perhaps debatable, conclusion. Remember we are finite beings attempting to understand an infinite God.

Depending on your theological bent, you may find other conclusions in this book questionable as well. A beauty of the Christian faith is that God has allowed room for a diversity of interpretations regarding non-essential doctrine. Non-essential refers to personal biblical understanding that does not alter the basis of salvation. Salvation is found in no one other than Jesus (see Acts 4:12). God's Gospel message is that He loves us and has given us His Son Jesus Christ as our only means of reconciliation with Him. "For God so loved the world that he gave his one and only Son, that whoever believes in him shall not perish but have eternal life" (John 3:16).

This book is not a study related to end-times theology, the tribulation period, or the millennial reign of Christ. I am choosing to focus on the experiences that follow death and the quality of life that lies beyond. Unless otherwise noted, all Biblical references come from the New International Version, 2011 Edition.

At many memorial services I have shared the wisdom of King Solomon who declared, "It is better to go to a house of mourning than to go to a house of feasting, for death is the destiny of everyone; the living should take this to heart" (Ecclesiastes 7:2). This statement has always grabbed attention. When I have spoken it at a memorial gathering, I have provided extra time for its truth to sink in. On the surface, it appears to be a falsehood, and amid grieving seems out of place, if not downright offensive.

The death of someone we know brings us face-to-face with our own mortality. A gift of memorial services and funerals, amongst other things, is that they bring about significant reflections on facing our own demise. In our consideration of the brevity of life, we are blessed if we direct our focus to God. This book attempts to lead the reader to deep reflection over his or her own mortality.

May you be enriched as you continue reading it and may you gain an accurate picture of what lies ahead.

CHAPTER 1 - SEEK THINGS ABOVE

"I would not give one moment of heaven for all the joy and riches of the world, even if it lasted for thousands and thousands of years."

Martin Luther

I have heard, and previously believed, the statement, "You can be so heavenly minded that you are of no earthly good." I do not remember when I first heard this or who I heard it from, but I have heard it stated many times by many people. A close parallel to this is to "Get your head out of the clouds." The reference encourages us to focus on the here and now without worrying, or even thinking, about the future. We are then motivated to focus on the tangible reality of this world without considering our future eternal realm.

The presumed wisdom of focusing only on the here (what we can see, touch, taste, and smell) originates with humankind. This focus contradicts the wisdom and guidance from God contained in the Bible. God encourages us, even commands us, to earnestly seek and strive for Heaven. The apostle Paul addressed this in his letter to the church in Colossae as he wrote, "Since, then, you have been raised with Christ, set (*zeteo*) your hearts on things above, where Christ is, seated at the right hand of God. Set (*phroneo*) your minds on things above, not on earthly things" (Colossians 3:1-2).

The Biblical author is communicating the opposite of the folk wisdom noted above. We are to be more heavenly minded, not less, and we are to be more heavenly hearted, not less. Once we understand that our focus needs to be more heavenly minded, then conversely, the more earthy good we can be. Like so many other teachings of the Bible, this truth turns worldly wisdom upside down.

The concept of setting, in the Greek word *zeteo*, refers to the action required of our hearts. In Paul's quote above, he uses this word when telling us to "set our hearts on things above". It appears in the present tense and speaks of an ongoing process. We are to keep seeking Heaven without stopping.

Jesus selected the word *zeteo* when He illustrated God's pursuit of seeking and reaching out to those who are spiritually lost. Jesus made the analogy of seeking out lost things that His audience could relate to and easily comprehend. Jesus used *zeteo* in speaking of the Shepherd who looks for lost sheep, the woman searching for a lost coin (see Luke 15:3-9), and the merchant searching for fine pearls (see Matthew 13:45). Likewise, we are instructed to keep on seeking Heaven and to never give up.

In contrast with his first use of *zeteo* for setting, the second time in the passage above, Paul changes the Greek word to *phroneo*. *Phroneo* is also is used in the present tense and speaks as well of an ongoing process with a slightly different understanding than *zeteo*. *Phroneo* instructs us to keep savoring, to keep fixated, or to keep considering, with our minds, in this case, focused on Heaven. This is the word Jesus also used to rebuke Peter's attempts to talk Him out of going to the cross. Peter was singularly caught up in human concerns. Jesus looked Peter in the eyes as he directly told him, "Get behind me, Satan! You are a stumbling block to me; you do not have in mind the concerns of God, but merely human concerns" (Matthew 16:23).

The instruction for us today is for our hearts and minds to center our lives in Christ. We are to make Him, His ways and His teaching that which our life revolves around. With our minds, we are to concentrate our concern on the eternal, not the temporal. This is not calling us to a life of irresponsibility, but rather to a life of priority. One way to seek things above is through prayer. Remember how Jesus taught us to pray? He starts, "Our Father who art *in Heaven*..." (Matthew 6:9). The Lord's prayer focuses our thoughts on Heaven. What a great prayer.

Pastoring is my second career. I earned a Bachelor of Science degree in Electrical Engineering Technology and worked either part time or full time in the high-tech electronic industry for 17 years. During that time, I came to the point where I placed my faith and my future into the hands of Jesus and received His forgiveness. My life was radically changed, and in honor of what Jesus had done for me, I began to give more of my time to volunteering in ministry at my local church.

The pastor of my church took notice of my dedication and invited me to resign from my job (and career path) and join his staff. At the time I had a fantastic job. It was high paying and included a sizeable stock package. The company was a reputable industry leader, and my role there fit me like a glove. My work was fruitful, enjoyable, and financially rewarding.

When challenged with the opportunity to start over in a new career, leave my area of expertise taking a significant reduction in pay, including the loss of stock equity, I needed guidance. I was fully aware that a transition into full-time ministry would require enrollment in a seminary to earn a master's degree. At the time, my wife and I were raising three young children. I was paralyzed not knowing what decision to make – to hang onto the seemingly secure job I had always dreamed of, atop the corporate ladder, or to leave it all and move into full-time ministry.

My reluctance to transition to full-time church work was firm because my heart and mind were too focused on earthly things. I had grown accustomed to my pay, my position, my power, and the prospects of early retirement. I was not sure that starting over in a new career, one so different from what I knew, was logical, practical or responsible.

Finding myself stuck, I was advised by my pastor Chip Ingram, to allow God to speak to me through His Word. I found the verse that I could anchor my decision to in Colossians 3:1-2. "Since, then, you have been raised with Christ, set your hearts on things above, where Christ is, seated at the right hand of God. Set your minds on things above, not on earthly things."

I had so much fear of "giving up" my skill set, my education, my career, my paycheck, and my identity that without this verse I would have remained in my old job. Looking back 26 years later, I am convinced that far from giving up; I instead traded up. God has given me the rare opportunity to study and teach the Bible and provide for my family in doing so. I am involved in helping people grow in their faith, and I could not imagine any use of my life to be more fulfilling than what it is now. And, though it has not always been easy, ever since I transitioned to be a full-time pastor, I have done a much better job of keeping my heart and mind focused on Heaven.

How do we continually seek after Heaven? The logical starting point to seeking Heaven is that we must have knowledge about the nature of Heaven. However, there are passages in Scripture, that appear to present obstacles from ever grasping or imagining what it will be like. Paul wrote an account of his experience from the perspective of the third person. He wrote, "I know a man in Christ who fourteen years ago was caught up to the third heaven. Whether it was in the body or out of the body, I do not know—God knows. And I know that this man—whether in the body or apart from the body I do not know, but God knows— was caught up to paradise and heard inexpressible things, things that no one is permitted to tell" (2 Corinthians 12:2-4).

The argument is made from this passage that a person cannot communicate that which is inexpressible. When Paul said that he was caught up to the third heaven and heard inexpressible things that he was not permitted to tell, perhaps these were things that God wanted only him to know. His persistent seeking after Heaven with his heart and mind allowed him to look beyond his present circumstances and accomplish significant advances for the Kingdom of God.

Paul, writing in his first letter to the church in Corinth had this to say about Heaven, "...as it is written: 'What no eye has seen, what no ear has heard, and what no human mind has conceived'— the things God has prepared for those who love him..." (1 Corinthians 2:9). This verse can be a stumbling block to human understanding for it communicates that the human heart and mind cannot begin to comprehend Heaven. The solution is found in the very next verse in this passage which states, "these are the things God has revealed to us by his Spirit" (1 Corinthians 2:10).

This verse provides hope and promise that if we search out what the Holy Spirit has revealed to us, we can gain knowledge and begin to understand Heaven. It is the Holy Spirit who brings the Scripture to life and helps humankind to draw out the meaning contained therein.

Paul's reference to "the third heaven" illuminates understanding about the nature of Heaven, particularly to thinkers in the Old and New Testament times. Easton's Bible Dictionary provides the Jewish notions that there were three heavens. The first heaven being our atmosphere – from the air we breathe to the clouds and blue sky we enjoy. The second heaven was the domain of the sun, moon, stars, and celestial planets. The third heaven was the home or dwelling place of God. Jesus referred to this in what is known as the Lord's prayer, "Our Father in heaven, hallowed be your name, your kingdom come, your will be done, on earth as it is in heaven" (Matthew 6:9-10).

We must consider that in various places the Bible does speak of Heaven using very familiar terms. Heaven is presented as a garden, a city, and a kingdom. Gardens, cities, and kingdoms are relatable to the human experience making Heaven at least somewhat familiar and understandable. So too the Bible mentions rooms, trees, vineyards, fruit, rivers, streets, and animals. These are described as being in Heaven, and these images offer us a bridge to initiate understanding, of what Heaven will be like.

Indeed, God does want us to know about Heaven as seen in His instructions to the Apostle John to detail his visit to Heaven. Through John's obedience to do so, we were given the book of Revelation. In addition to John's details, the visions seen by the prophets Isaiah and Ezekiel concerning Heaven are preserved in writings attributed to their names (See Isaiah Chapters 65,66 and Ezekiel Chapters 1-3, 33-48).

As you read on, you will learn, among other things, that at death your body returns to dust, your spirit returns to God, your faith will be confirmed, and you will consciously (yet temporarily) dwell in either Paradise or Hades. As we explore Heaven further, we will learn that "you" in the next life, will be the same "you" as in this life, with the same recognizable personality and memories. You will not be a stranger to yourself, or to anyone you knew in your first life either.

The Bible helps us to see that the questions of what *is* Heaven like now, and what *will* Heaven be like have two different answers. As we will see, Paradise, the new home promised to the thief who died alongside Jesus, is intermediate. Only after Jesus returns and our bodies are resurrected, will we be moved into our final Heavenly destination. In Paradise, we will have temporal bodies. In Heaven, we will have our resurrected bodies, located in the resurrected (made new) Earth.

Peter addressed this when he wrote, "But in keeping with his promise we are looking forward to a new heaven and a new earth, where righteousness dwells" (2 Peter 3:13).

When the New Heaven and New Earth are restored, they will come together; and Paradise, our interim dwelling place, will become the New Heaven which will become the New Earth. Once again, as in the Genesis creation account, humankind and God will dwell together. We can call that dwelling place the New Heaven, or we can call it the New Earth. They will be one and the same.

In the end, the world will be as God designed it to be, a place of eternal bliss and purpose where God and man will dwell together forever. We can know about Heaven because the Bible pulls back the curtain and allows us to peek inside.

The remainder of this book gives more specifics about what awaits. I encourage you to make the most of this life while you still possess it. Begin today to anticipate and prepare for heaven eagerly. Starting today, why not make the shift to diligently, actively and single-mindedly set your hearts on things above? Let your mind begin fixating, savoring and continually dwelling upon eternity above. Bring this topic up in your conversations and find scriptural books to read concerning Heaven.

I highly recommend a couple of books in the bibliography included at the end of this book. Ask God to give you dreams about Heaven and the life that awaits. Many of us have not because we ask not. Whatever you do, however, embrace the encouragement to become more Heavenly focused. You will find that you become earthlier good as you do so.

CHAPTER 2 - LIFE IS SHORT, THEN WE DIE

"There comes a moment when we all must realize that life is short, and in the end the only thing that really counts is not how others see us, but how God sees us."

Billy Graham

We have come to accept that death is natural and to be expected once we hit old age. How many times have you heard the phrase, "He or she died of natural causes?" Likewise, we are inclined to find comfort in speaking of those who have lived 90 or more years as having enjoyed a long life. This is like saying it's okay that they died, at least they lived many years. It seems like we are very adept at attempting to take the sting out of death.

As I was writing this book, I officiated over the graveside burial of a 94-year-old World War II veteran. This was a man, who 33 years earlier, placed his faith in Jesus, and it was with the greatest of confidence his family declared that he was now with Jesus in Paradise. Sadly, he is buried not only with his wife in a double stacked grave, but also ten yards away from where his 21-year-old grandson is buried. (This was a young man whose memorial service I had officiated 4 years earlier.) By their confession of faith, all three members of this family are in Heaven. Yet to their relatives, death, at any age causes tears to flow.

We are disturbed when the "natural" occurrence of death is hastened through things such as cancer, heart attack, disease, homicide, suicide, violence, and accident. It has become easier to accept the death of an octogenarian or older person while viewing the death of someone younger as tragic or senseless. Yet all death is tragic! Every single death is a tragedy. Death is not a part of God's original design; for neither human beings nor animals.

Humankind was created by God and placed into the Garden of Eden to live forever with Him, in a state of continual purpose and bliss. Death only arrived after sin appeared, as a forewarned penalty (see Genesis 2:17). Whether we live to be 10 or 110, this time is minuscule considering eternity. God has so much more in mind for us.

The brevity of life is something we must all contend with. The older we are, the faster it seems time is slipping away. Consider the words of Moses, the liberator of the Hebrew captives: "Our days may come to seventy years, or eighty, if our strength endures; yet the best of them are but trouble and sorrow, for they quickly pass, and we fly away" (Psalm 90:10).

Wait a minute, I object! I have had some pretty good days in my life. How could my wedding day, the birthdays of my three children, the celebration of my parents 50th anniversary, the weddings of my three children, or vacationing in Europe, be considered full of trouble and sorrow? The only possible answer is found by comparing this life to the next. Relatively speaking, every day of this life is filled with stress and pain as compared to what it will be for those who go to Heaven.

Regardless of good or bad, our days quickly pass. Again, Moses states, "Yet you sweep people away in the sleep of death—they are like the new grass of the morning: In the morning it springs up new, but by evening it is dry and withered" (Psalm 90:5-6).

King David made a similar assertion when he wrote, "The life of mortals is like grass, they flourish like a flower of the field; the wind blows over it, and it is gone, and its place remembers it no more" (Psalm 103:15-16).

The Apostle Peter also understood the shortness of life as he recorded; "For, 'All people are like grass, and all their glory is like the flowers of the field; the grass withers and the flowers fall, but the word of the Lord endures forever" (1 Peter 1:24-25).

Have we ever considered our present life to be like cut flowers? A fresh bouquet smells great and looks great, but those same flowers are in the process of decay. So are we.

Moses gave us his thesis on the brevity of life when he wrote Psalm 90; take note of his appeal: "If only we knew the power of your anger! Your wrath is as great as the fear that is your due. Teach us to number our days, that we may gain a heart of wisdom" (Psalm 90:11-12).

God's anger and wrath are being stored up against sin which has marred His creation. The wrath of God's power is something none of us want to encounter. Understanding more about sin, the Curse of sin, the fall of mankind and the redemption of God is foundational to living with the hope of Heaven. Even reading this simple book is a great way to begin looking at death, counting your days (life is short), and gaining a heart of wisdom.

One of mankind's most significant dilemmas is that we have a deep-seated desire in our hearts to live forever, yet we are cut off from the life we know and cherish by the cruelty of death. The human condition, and the seeking after of hope, have been debated for centuries by religious leaders, theologians, and philosophers alike. We have been captivated by stories of the "fountain of youth" and have sought satisfying answers to living forever whether true or not.

The multitude of beliefs held regarding life after death varies widely. Many of these beliefs are contradictory when compared with each other. All the views may be wrong, but they cannot all be correct. Our sincere search for truth requires this exclusivity principle to define reality. Many people "cherry pick" various elements within different belief systems to establish their own understanding of death. We have a responsibility, as best we can, to remove wishful thinking related to death. This is what the Bible provides.

18

Death is man's greatest enemy. A multitude of conversations I have had leads me to assume that most people want to experience more than just this life. A common understanding of life after death, or "Heaven" may not be shared, yet people long to live forever. Unfortunately, more than longing is needed to get there. No matter how hard we may believe in a specific outcome when we die, we cannot create our own reality. Reality is found in Truth which is beyond the realm of our wishful thinking.

The source of all truth is found in the Bible. The Apostle John declared, "Sanctify them by the truth; your word is truth" (John 17:17). To be sanctified is to be set apart. The Bible does present a distinct path to Heaven, set apart from all other religions and philosophies.

All beliefs originate from somewhere. They come from the minds of great thinkers, the writings of the founders of religions, and from ancient traditions and teachings handed down through the ages. Whatever you currently believe about death and the afterlife originated with someone who came before. This book presents a view on death and immortality taken from my own study of the Bible. I have also been influenced by Randy Alcorn's book *Heaven,* and John Eldridge's book, *All Things New.*

Death is far too important a subject to misunderstand. Where then, shall we place our confidence? When it comes to death, we must seek after the correct understanding. So many of life's problems and answers are yielded to the authority of a created, adapted or copied belief system. We are well served to pick a belief system with a solid foundation. When it comes to death, we want to get it right. The stakes are far too high to do otherwise, or to leave the outcome to chance.

I am suggesting that we turn to the Holy Scriptures for answers, and I understand that this is challenging for some. Hurdles include bias, for example: that the Bible is a compilation of man-made stories, full of inconsistencies and contradictions. The Bible may have been misapplied, misunderstood or used in a self-serving manner to control or harm. Perhaps someone has represented teaching "from the Bible" that it does not contain, or proposed a truth never substantiated with Chapter and verse.

Since death is mankind's greatest certainty, we need to discover for ourselves what the Bible has to say about the subject. We then get to decide if what the Word of God presents merits our trust and faith.

My perspective of the Bible has changed dramatically over my lifetime. I went from being a skeptic, and one who thought the Bible was entirely irrelevant to life, to a person who has committed his life to follow and apply its teachings. I looked for answers to the meaning of life while observing other Bible-based believers. This inspired me to open my heart and mind to what the Bible revealed. Over these last 30 years, my convictions in trusting the Bible have become stronger as I have learned more about this fantastic, one of a kind book.

The Bible is the most widely printed, distributed, and read book in all of history.[1] Every attempt made to destroy it has failed. It comes with the undeniable power of authentic life change. It was written by forty different people known for their godliness, over hundreds of years, yet contained within is a unified theme. The Bible has been translated into more languages than any other book[2], and throughout the generations, it has been accepted and authenticated as indeed a life-changing book.

Countless souls have been sacrificed defending it and spreading its message. Perhaps most interesting is that the Bible repeatedly claims to be the Word of God. Arguments opposed to it, and attempts to eliminate it, have not endured. I invite us to allow its teaching about death and the afterlife to stimulate our thinking and shape our views. Remember, we do have the choice to decide for ourselves what to believe and why. My challenge is to ask for a fair hearing to what the Bible has to say.

Before exploring what is taught in the Bible about life after death, here are seven of the most popular non-Biblical views. They are simplistically presented to give us a contrast to what the Bible declares.

1. <u>Annihilation</u>

Annihilation is the view that this life is all there is; at death, life is obliterated. Nothing follows. The body, the physical part of a person, and the spirit, the nonphysical part of a person which includes the seat of emotions, character and the divine nature within, cease to exist. Life does not continue, no soul remains, and no spirit is released. Death is the final Chapter in our short, and perhaps meaningless, life on this earth. Considering how vast the universe is, our lives really are small and insignificant. Yes, the memory of us may live on through others. Depending on our achievements, our legacy may live on in the history books. But ultimately, given enough time, we are forgotten, books are lost or destroyed, and so are all memories of us.

2. Soul-Sleep

Soul-sleep is the teaching that when a person dies that their soul "sleeps" until the time of the future resurrection. In this condition, the person is not aware or conscious. Soul-sleep is a belief in a place of utter calmness and darkness to which the dead are assigned. Independent of the moral choices made in this life, are cut off from all experience and from God. The righteous and the unrighteous, the good and the not-so-good. Sleep is associated with the separation of your problems and worries, a place where rest is finally achieved. Those who refer to "resting in peace" (RIP) often think of soul-sleep. In this state, we are without strength and without personality, but this is distinct from being annihilated.

A passage in the Old Testament is sometimes used to justify belief in soul-sleep. The story of King Saul contacting the deceased prophet Samuel, though the medium (or witch) of Endor is often cited. King Saul relied upon Samuel to receive guidance from God. Thus, when the prophet died, he was left not knowing what to do. To remedy the situation, he enquired of a medium in the town of Endor and asked her to bring up Samuel from the dead that he might consult him one more time. She was able to do this, and when Samuel came up out of the earth as a ghostly figure, he asked why King Saul had disturbed him, presumably from sleep (see 1 Samuel 28).

This happens to be one of those captivating stories in the Old Testament that validates the reality of a medium's ability to contact the dead, yet it does not provide adequate proof to establish the belief in indefinite soul-sleep. Based on King Saul's experience, the practice of conjuring up spirits holds some validity, though Biblically it is forbidden.

Moses, the author of the Old Testament Book of Deuteronomy, wrote, "Let no one be found among you ... who practices divination or sorcery, interprets omens, engages in witchcraft, or casts spells, or who is a medium or spiritist or who consults the dead. Anyone who does these things is detestable to the Lord..." (Deuteronomy 10:10-12).

Just because an experience like Saul's may have occurred, that does not establish the grounds for the reliability of the practice to conjure up the dead for answers to life. A life and death belief system impacting eternity demands a foundation stronger and more reliable than experience alone. Remember, we have a living God to inquire of as the Prophet Isaiah reported, "When someone tells you to consult mediums and spiritists, who whisper and mutter, should not a people inquire of their God? Why consult the dead on behalf of the living?" (Isaiah 8:19).

3. Reincarnation

A third belief system is Reincarnation. This suggests a new life after this one expires, but in a different physical body or form (human to human, animal to human, human to animal). It is both a philosophical view and a religious view based on the thought of cyclical existence. This belief is held as a significant tenet of faith in many of the Eastern Religions – Buddhism, Hinduism and Sikhism. The appeal of reincarnation is that we are never placed into this world accidentally. We were born into this world with a purpose and a mission. In Buddhism, the present Earth is thought of as a foreign school, visited for short periods for spiritual training.[3]

The Wiccan Occult embraces a form of reincarnation. They hold that souls rest and recuperate in a placed called the Summerland. They are then reincarnated but lose all memory of their prior life. Those holding a view of reincarnation believe the universe is stuck in a cycle of endless recurrence.

Suffering is a part of the recurrence of reincarnation. The goal, after an indeterminable number of reincarnations, is to achieve Nirvana, a term used in Hinduism. Nirvana is achieved when an understanding of the relationship between God and man is achieved. Only after Nirvana is achieved will the afterlife, rather than reincarnation, occur.[4]

4. **Purgatory**

A widespread belief is the concept of Purgatory. The Catechism of the Catholic Church teaches, "All who die in God's grace and friendship, but still imperfectly purified, are indeed assured of their eternal salvation; but after death, they undergo purification, to achieve the holiness necessary to enter in the joy of Heaven."[5] This teaching has come from the longstanding tradition of the Roman Catholic Church and the practice of prayer for the dead mentioned in the Apocrypha.[6]

The doctrine of Purgatory is uniquely different from reincarnation in that this is not a complete rebirth; instead, it teaches a holding place of mild to moderate punishment with purifying fire. This belief is best understood as a continuation of works, or merit, to achieve the necessary holiness to enter Heaven. Purgatory exists because Jesus' death is deemed insufficiently adequate to purify a person from all their sins. His death took care of some of our sins, but not all of them. This is contrary to what the Bible teaches.

5. **Works-based Eternal Pleasure or Pain**

Humanists believe that eternal pleasure or pain is based on the net outcome of each person's life. Because this view holds that life is "works" based, it becomes a matter of having the sum of all our good deeds outweigh the sum of all our bad deeds. It holds to a belief that "god" grades on a curve and what is all important is to get a "passing grade." One may never know how their efforts are viewed in the sight of deity so the assurance of their eternal resting place may remain hidden until death. Most significantly however, is that this belief means that Jesus died unnecessarily.

6. <u>Universalism</u>

Universalism holds that all souls will ultimately be saved and that there are no torments of Hell. A foundational belief is that God's love is so strong and pure that He could never send anyone to Hell. This is a fatalistic perspective presented in a positive light. The outcome is good for everyone, both sinner and saint. Our fate is already sealed, and the result is that everyone will go to Heaven. I hear this perspective commonly shared; seldom have I heard anyone speak of eternal punishment in Hell. Nor have I attended a funeral or memorial service where it was spoken publicly that the bereaved is now most likely in Hell.

7. <u>Impossible to Know</u>

Finally, there are those who hold that what happens after death is guesswork, leaving uncertainty about what happens beyond this life. With this understanding, it is impossible to definitively know what happens after death, even though stories of NDE's (near death experiences) are often documented.

Near death experiences, or NDE's (people dying and then coming back from the dead), have captured our imaginations and, in many cases, have become the new "bible" on death. As individual experiences, which can be fabricated, NDE's are subject to misleading deception.

Take Alex Malarkey and his book, *The Boy Who Came Back From Heaven* for example. Despite selling over 1 million copies and appearing for months on the New York Times bestseller's list, his story of going to heaven and meeting Jesus was later retracted. It was admitted that the entire story was fabricated. The book is now removed from publication.[7]

In an astonishing admittance of fabrication, Alex wrote, *"Please forgive the brevity, but because of my limitations, I have to keep this short. I did not die. I did not go to Heaven. I said I went to Heaven because I thought it would get me attention. When I made the claims that I did, I had never read the Bible. People have profited from lies and continue to. They should read the Bible, which is enough. The Bible is the only source of truth. Anything written by man cannot be infallible. It is only through repentance of your sins and a belief in Jesus as the Son of God, who died for your sins (even though he committed none of his own) so that you can be forgiven may you learn of Heaven outside of what is written in the Bible... not by reading a work of man. I want the whole world to know that the Bible is sufficient. Those who market these materials must be called to repent and hold the Bible as enough. In Christ, Alex Malarkey."*[8]

As you can see, there are numerous non-Biblical views on life beyond. It seems reasonable that a God who loves us would want to provide clear directions on how to get to where He says we will go, and what it is like there. All that claim that God is love are correct. A loving

God would want what is best for his prized creation. As such, God would be expected to make His will and ways known. This is what the written Word of God accomplishes. All else is guesswork and guesswork is a sure means to end up being wrong.

CHAPTER 3 - WHAT HAPPENS WHEN WE DIE?

"While I thought that I was learning how to live, I have been learning how to die."

Leonardo da Vinci

We make many decisions in life. Our journey is full of twists and turns. In this life we need to determine educational goals, career paths, housing options, and locations, whether to marry and to whom – plus hundreds more. But, since at death, our fate is sealed, the most important decision we make in this life relates to how we respond to Jesus and His offer of eternal life.

We are made aware that "God is not the author of confusion" (1 Corinthians 14:33 NKJV). He does not want anyone confused or misled on what happens after we die. Instead, He wants to prepare us for what comes next.

The topic of death is routinely either avoided, dismissed or dreaded. We should note that the biblical concept of death is one of separation, not cessation. Death separates us from our loved ones, from our bodies, and life as we know it on this earth. Death is the ultimate separator which in part is why it is so painful. Separation implies loss – loss of contact, of communication, of touch, of sharing. Cessation suggests coming to the very end; ceasing to exist any longer. Biblically, death is never referred to as an ending.

Death is a fearsome enemy. The pure awareness of it causes many to question when it will happen. The website www.deathclock.com allows you to enter your birthday and gender and then it reports the day you will most likely die based on death statistics.

Many of us wonder about the way we will die and if there will be pain involved. Accounts from those who nearly drowned or froze to death, who became unconscious but were later revived, describe the experience as peacefully falling asleep – once they let go. We long to know if the process of dying will come quickly or if, it will be prolonged.

With vivid images seared into my memory, I recall being present when others have experienced raw grief when confronted with the shockwave of the death of a loved one. I have stood at the side of a 6 foot by 3 foot by 6-foot-deep perfectly shaped rectangular hole as parents have lowered the casket of their 9-year-old daughter into the grave. I have received the frantic call of a wife who had just witnessed her husband being struck and killed while riding on his motorcycle, as she was riding, following behind him. I have been at the side of a father in the hospital with his 20-year-old daughter who had fallen ill and then lying breathless in the adjacent room as he desperately tried for hours to reach his wife. When finally, she arrived, I will never forget her dropping to her knees and wailing bitterly. I have come alongside many family members, doing my best to help them accept their new reality. Death is ugly, and death is painful; it is mankind's greatest enemy.

Death stings. However, Jesus takes on that pain for us. The Apostle Paul, fully aware of the resurrection that waits for those who trust in the Lord proclaimed, "Where, O death, is your victory? Where, O death, is your sting?" (1 Corinthians 15:55).

To gain Paul's perspective, we must turn to the opening pages of the Bible. The first two Chapters in Genesis tell of the creation of the universe and everything in it. The pattern of creation was that God spoke and at the power of His Word, that which had not been, came into existence, and God declared it to be good. The pinnacle of creation was man, who was formed from the dust of the ground (see Genesis 2:7).

God fashioned humankind, both male and female into their present form, much like a potter shapes a piece of clay into its intended design. God then breathed the breath of life into their nostrils, making them living beings. Living beings, which as noted earlier, were intended to live forever with God in the Garden of Eden, a place also known as Paradise.

God created humankind with the dignity of free will, capable of making choices. Of course, God longed for them to use their freedom to make decisions which would demonstrate love toward Him, their Creator.

Some measure of obedience, enabled through free choice, was needed. Therefore, God placed a tree with forbidden fruit, the tree of the knowledge of good and evil, in the Garden of Eden with the prohibition not to eat of its fruit. It was not a difficult command to follow. There was an unlimited source of food; most notably the sweet fruit from the beautiful tree of life.

The single prohibition came with a warning that to choose not to listen, and to disobey God, would invoke the severest of penalties; death. The result would be separation from God. Three Chapters into the Bible Adam and Eve were tempted to eat the forbidden fruit. They succumbed to temptation. Disobedience ushered death and other consequences into the human experience.

God declared, "By the sweat of your brow you will eat your food until you return to the ground, since from it you were taken; for dust you are and to dust you will return" (Genesis 3:19). King Solomon reminded us of this penalty when he stated, "All go to the same place; all come from dust, and to dust all return" (Ecclesiastes 3:20).

From the biblical account of creation, we are made aware that we came from dust, and at death, we will return to dust. Out of tradition, or personal preference, some choose casket burial for our bodies, while others select cremation. Yet, no matter how our body is disposed of, there is nothing we can do to prevent its decay and return to dust.

As a pastor, I am often asked about cremation: Is there a preference of casket burial over cremation, or a biblical prohibition against cremation? The Bible makes it understandable that our bodies will one day be resurrected, and we have the freedom to choose our final arrangements.

Some may think cremation hinders God's future ability to resurrect our bodies and is offensive to God but remember, "with God all things are possible" (Matthew 19:26). The belief that our resurrection requires intact bodily remains, is problematic. What then would become of those incinerated in a fire, lost and drowned at sea, blown apart in an explosion, or destroyed in a terrible accident? God can do the impossible, and for us to be resurrected, He does not need our "dust" to be neatly stored in a human-made box.

We find accounts of cremation in the Bible. The greedy Israelite soldier, Achan, disobeyed Joshua and took plunder from the enemy for his provision. As a result of not only disobeying Joshua, but God also, Achan was removed from the camp, stoned to death and then cremated (see Joshua 7:25). King Saul also was cremated (see 1 Samuel 31:12).

There is no indication in the Bible that on the last day when the resurrection takes place there are any exception clauses for bodies which will not be raised back to life. Those who are buried, cremated or lost at sea, just like those buried in caskets, will be provided their resurrected bodies in the life beyond.

The Scriptures state that the day will come when God, "... will send his angels and gather his elect (those who will go to Heaven) from the four winds, from the ends of the earth to the ends of the heavens" (Mark 13:27). It is possible that the dust I am made of, the dust we all are made of, may be scattered across the globe and yet this will not keep God from resurrecting anyone's body.

Since, at death, the body returns to dust, one may wonder where the spirit placed within man goes. King Solomon gives us the answer, "... the dust returns to the ground it came from, and the spirit returns to God who gave it" (Ecclesiastes 12:7).

The spirit of all who live returns to the Giver of life immediately after their last breath on Earth is taken. The human spirit does not necessarily remain with God; it either remains with God or is banished from God's presence. The determining factor is whether we have believed in Jesus and His substitutionary death for our sins.

The writer of the book of Hebrews states, "... people are destined to die once, and after that to face judgment" (Hebrews 9:27). When our spirit appears in the presence of God, our faith will be exposed for what it has been. There will be no hiding from God what our hearts and minds held to be true. To be clear, apart from the guaranteed return of Jesus, all who live will die. At death your fate is sealed, your body will return to dust (temporarily), and your spirit will return to God who gave it. The judgment of your faith that happens next will confirm your eternal destiny.

If we are discovered to have received God's forgiveness of our sin, we will remain with God forever. However, if we are found to be unforgiven of our sin, we will be banished from God's presence forever. The determining factor is our response *in this life* to the Gospel (good news) message.

To understand the Gospel, it is imperative that we grasp that death is not natural. Instead, "the wages of sin is death" (Romans 6:23). Furthermore, we must comprehend that all have sinned. The Apostle Paul declares that "All have sinned and fall short of the glory of God" (Romans 3:23). If that was not clear enough, under the inspiration of the Holy Spirit, he also wrote, "There is no one righteous, not even one; ... there is no one who does good, not even one" (Romans 3:10-12).

Sin results in the death (forever separation) of humans from God; a chasm too vast to span by our good works and good deeds. The only way for reconciliation between God and humankind to occur is for God to take away our sin.

Jesus Christ, being fully God and fully man, lived the only perfectly sinless life in all human history. As John the Baptist proclaimed, "He came to take away the sin of the world" (John 1:29). The Apostle Paul writes, "God made him who had no sin to be sin for us, so that in him we might become the righteousness of God" (2 Corinthians 5:21).

As noted, Adam and Eve disobeyed God and brought sin into the world. The penalty for this was separation from God, a fundamental change in the nature of humanity to that of an inherited sin nature, and ultimately death. Jesus paid the full penalty by dying on the cross. He defeated sin and death. God then, mercifully executed His plan to reconcile with humankind and heal the separation. God's grace gave us Jesus who took on our sins and paid the full penalty price for them, by dying on the cross. After He was buried, He conquered death and sin by the resurrection from the grave three days later. Jesus completely destroyed death and its causation, sin (see 1 Corinthians 15:1-4).

Through His death Jesus has offered us the gift of eternal life; this is granted by His grace and not something we can merit on our own.[9] Those who believe this message will never be put to shame.[10] They will be saved from an eternity apart from God.[11] Moreover, they will have the right to be called children of God.[12] And they will have eternal life with Jesus after passing from death to life.[13]

On the day Jesus died, he was the middle man, placed between two-lifetime criminals. The one thief recognized Jesus to be who He said he was and confessed his faith in Jesus, accepting Him as His Savior mere minutes before he died. This criminal was nailed to his own cross and could not lift hand or foot to do anything for God. Yet he was promised entrance into Paradise (see Luke 23:39-43).

God is generous. He offers eternal life based solely on His merit and not ours. Jesus is the middle man who stands between a Holy God and sinful man. Salvation is not earned. Those who think that they can impress God by their goodness, deny the pain that Jesus endured and thereby nullify His death. Salvation is a gift.

I invite you to pause. If what you just read makes no sense to you then I encourage you to take the few minutes necessary to go back and re-read the last two pages. If comprehension of what I am attempting to communicate still doesn't make sense, then may I suggest that you pray to God for understanding. There is no more important message to consider than the message of salvation in determining your eternal destiny. The stakes are high, and the offer of life is knocking at your door.

Imagine yourself on the day of your judgment of faith: You are standing before your Creator. God is looking straight at you, and instead of seeing your misdeeds He sees only the righteousness of His son, Jesus. Indeed, that is good news! When our sin is forgiven, it is remembered no more (see Hebrews 10:17). The purity of Jesus, His holiness, and His righteousness are credited to us. Credited righteousness is the theme of the book of Romans Chapter 4 which makes for an inspiring read.

Once we have accepted Christ's atoning death on our behalf our name will be written in the Lamb's Book of Life. The judgment of faith we undergo will be a matter of God finding, or not finding, our name in that Book. If we have rejected Jesus Christ and his offer of forgiveness, our name will never be found. More will be shared on this subject later.

CHAPTER 4 - THE STORY OF TWO DEAD PEOPLE

"What good is it for someone to gain the whole world, yet forfeit their soul?"

Jesus Christ

Accounts of near-death experiences (NDE's) are numerous, and they have a way of grabbing our attention. A search on Amazon yields more than 100 books on personal near-death experiences and literally hundreds of NDE videos can be found on YouTube. We are intrigued by knowing the possibilities of what to expect on the other side of death. Outside of what the Bible reveals to us of our next life, we seem to be anxious to learn whatever we can from every source imaginable, especially the supernatural.

Near death experiences (dying and then coming back from the dead) have common elements. Traveling through a tunnel of light, (sometimes at very high speeds), encountering a god-like supernatural being, intense emotions of either love and peace or fear and horror, along with a review of one's life are recounted. People often report seeing their lives flash before them.

As fascinating as these stories are, Jesus provides a credible account of two human beings who had died, and what their "life beyond" experience entailed.

Jesus was a masterful storyteller, who had a unique way of conveying spiritual truth to those who genuinely sought it. He often narrated in short stories with a significant impact; parables. But not all his stories were parables; or allegories. In the Gospel, according to Luke, he told the real-life and death, situation of two dead people.

In this true story, He pulled back the curtain and allowed his audience to see two individuals, a nameless wealthy man and a beggar named Lazarus, who ended up in two distinct locations:

"There was a rich man who was dressed in purple and fine linen and lived in luxury every day. At his gate was laid a beggar named Lazarus, covered with sores and longing to eat what fell from the rich man's table. Even the dogs came and licked his sores. The time came when the beggar died, and the angels carried him to Abraham's side. The rich man also died and was buried. In Hades, where he was in torment, he looked up and saw Abraham far away, with Lazarus by his side. So he called to him, 'Father Abraham, have pity on me and send Lazarus to dip the tip of his finger in water and cool my tongue, because I am in agony in this fire.' But Abraham replied, 'Son, remember that in your lifetime you received your good things, while Lazarus received bad things, but now he is comforted here and you are in agony. And besides all this, between us and you a great chasm has been set in place, so that those who want to go from here to you cannot, nor can anyone cross over from there to us.' He answered, 'Then I beg you, father, send Lazarus to my family, for I have five brothers. Let him warn them, so that they will not also come to this place of torment.' Abraham replied, 'They have Moses and the Prophets; let them listen to them.' 'No, father Abraham,' he said, 'but if someone from the dead goes to them, they will repent.' He said to him, 'If they do not listen to Moses and the Prophets, they will not be convinced even if someone rises from the dead.'" (Luke 16:19-31).

As in the death of all people, we can assume from this account in Luke 16, that the bodies of the rich man and the beggar, began the process of decay (returning to dirt). Their spirits returned to God as King Solomon declared: "and the dust returns to the ground it came from, and the spirit returns to God who gave it" (Ecclesiastes 12:7). Since they ended up in two distinct places, we can surmise that their lives were evaluated by God before they were assigned their eternal home. (We will consider the judgment of the dead later in this book.)

Due to their economic status at the time, it is likely that Lazarus, the poor beggar, was thrown into the city dump, a place called Gehenna, where a fire burned continuously and consumed trash as well as the bodies of dead animals, poor people, and even some criminals. A place for the forgotten. The rich man, on the other hand, likely had an expensive funeral where his life was remembered, mourned, and celebrated. This was a man who lived in comfort and security. In contrast, the disabled beggar was pitiful, living in extreme poverty and scrounging for whatever scrap morsels of food he could get his hands on. Their difference in life was as stark as it was in death. These two men were at opposite ends of the social-economic spectrum.

What is unique about this story, as compared to Jesus' parables is that he names one of the individuals – the poor beggar Lazarus. Jesus does not name any of the characters in His other parables. For example, we do not know the name of the prodigal son (or his father and brother), we do not know the name of the farmer who scattered seeds, and we do not know the name of the persistent widow. If this story were a parable, we would wonder why Jesus broke with his custom of assigning names to the characters. If Lazarus were a fabricated name that Jesus chose, then it would be an extraordinary and troubling choice because of another Biblical "Lazarus."

The other Lazarus was one of Jesus' best friends, a man who had also died but was miraculously brought back to life by Jesus as recorded in John Chapter 11. Lazarus, the friend of Jesus, was a rich man, while the Lazarus from our earlier story, was a poor beggar. Willfully using the same name could be confusing if it were not true. The best explanation for using the name Lazarus is that this was an actual person, and Lazarus was his real name.

A glimpse into this story reveals several truths upon which we can begin to shape and mold our Biblical understanding of life after death. Seven significant observations from this story can be seen:

1. <u>The Important Role of Angels</u>

When the beggar died, angels carried him to Abraham's side. The accompaniment of angels is consistent with what the Bible tells us about having a role in the death of humans. Angels are sent to gather the dead from the ends of the earth (see Mark 13:27). According to Psalm 103, which speaks of God's redemptive power, it is the angels who do God's bidding (see Psalm 103:20). Gathered together with loved ones, I have been at the bedside of individuals at the moment they have passed from this life to the next. It is common for a person to open their eyes and smile immediately before they die as though they see some celestial being or angel. I have heard similar stories from Hospice nurses; some say that the person dying has even called attention to the unseen angels that are present in the room.

We are told that at the return of Christ, also known as His second coming, angels will be active in arousing and gathering those who sleep in death. "At that time people will see the Son of Man coming in clouds with great power and glory. And he will send his angels and gather his elect from the four winds, from the ends of the earth to the ends of the heavens" (Mark 13:26-27). The fact that an angel is mentioned in the story of Lazarus and the rich man gives credence to its reliability as being true.

2. Old Testament Sheol was Compartmentalized

At this time in Jewish history, the deceased were said to go to Sheol, the place of the dead and the Old Testament word for the Beyond, also known as the "common receptacle" for the dead. This story makes it clear, however, that Sheol was compartmentalized because one of the locations was referred to as "Abraham's Bosom" – some translations state "Abraham's Side" – (another word for Paradise) while the other location was a place of torment often referred to as Hades. Both locations reflect an environment where the occupants are conscious of their surroundings, fully aware of their status, and placed in a setting they cannot escape. These details indicate that Lazarus and the rich man had direct continuity from this life to the next. The pain the rich man experienced, mentioned four times as either torment or agony, is a form of punishment[14] indicating the suffering is very real.

3. Transitional Bodies

Lazarus and the rich man do not appear to be disembodied spirits, but instead, they have some sort of transitional body or physical form. This passage speaks of thirst, pain, tongue, finger, and sight which require a body to experience, even though there is no indication that their bodies had yet to be resurrected or restored to life after the grave. The rich man viewed his request to be comforted as a reasonable request, which Abraham decisively turned down.

4. The Importance of Decisions

The decisions we make in this life follow us to the next. In this life, we have the freedom to make our decisions, but then our decisions ultimately define us. The fact that water was available and that physical forms are mentioned suggest a physical, multi-dimensional place. This is important to note as some scholars teach that the dead will be disembodied spirits until the resurrection of the bodies of the dead. These two, who knew each other in life, also recognized each other in death and likewise recognized Father Abraham. Clearly, they knew one another. In their dialogue, they reasoned and communicated and maintained their distinct identities formed on Earth.

5. The Isolation of Hades

Lazarus is carried by angels to be with Abraham and is later seen by the rich man standing by Abraham's side. By inference, the rich man is by himself. Some think Hell's consolation prize will be fellowship with other sinners. People have told me that they would rather go to Hell so that they could hang out in bars, listen to loud music, get drunk and shoot pool with their friends than go to Heaven. They mistakenly view Heaven as boring; a place with very little fun. Created as relational beings, we are made for each other and isolation adds to the torment of the ungodly. In Hades people are shut out from all of God's goodness, which includes the relationships He provides. There will be no comfort, no consolation for those in Hades. The isolation and torment of Hades are that of Hell. Like men and women

45

incarcerated in prisons who dread solitary confinement and describe it as a living Hell.[15]

6. Memory in the Afterlife

The rich man certainly remembers his brothers and possibly sees them. He expresses compassion for them and longs to warn them to do whatever is necessary to avoid his demise. Memory appears to remain intact and is not taken from him. Our minds and memories help make us who we are as people. The fact that the rich man cares, shows that this man was not wholly evil; perhaps he was merely indifferent to the plight of the extreme poor. We must note that Hell will be filled with many "good people" – the determining factor of where we end up is not our morality, but our response to Jesus Christ's substitutionary death on our behalf – the Gospel message.

7. The Fixed Chasm

Lastly, we are told in the poor beggar's story that there is a fixed chasm separating Abraham's Bosom and Hades which no one can cross. At death, the destiny of the rich man and Lazarus was secured. There was no possibility of reincarnation and no possibility of a second chance. These Scriptures speak to the finality of death and the urgent importance of understanding all that we can about what happens before experiencing it.

Remember, this is an event told by Jesus; an account that clearly indicates people can end up in a place of eternal torment. Not all people do. Yet, we have been falsely introduced to a God who is so loving and kind that we imagine He could NEVER consign anyone to Hell and eternal punishment. To this Peter says that God "is patient with you, not wanting anyone to perish, but everyone to come to repentance" (2 Peter 3:9).

God does not send anyone to Hell. We are the ones who send ourselves there through our stubborn unbelief. To not choose to accept Jesus' offer of salvation is to choose against Him. As the Apostle John declared, "Whoever believes in him is not condemned, but whoever does not believe stands condemned already because they have not believed in the name of God's one and only Son" (John 3:18).

What about the infant or young child that cannot rationalize this truth? Are they to be consigned to Hell? Or what about the fate of an aborted child? To these questions, one must understand that the Bible speaks of life beginning at conception.

"For you created my inmost being; you knit me together in my mother's womb. I praise you because I am fearfully and wonderfully made; your works are wonderful, I know that full well. My frame was not hidden from you when I was made in the secret place, when I was woven together in the depths of the earth. Your eyes saw my unformed body; all the days ordained for me were written in your book before one of them came to be" (Psalm 139:13-16).

A prenatal mind, an infant mind, and even a toddler's mind is incapable of comprehending sin and its consequences. The young mind is also unable to grasp the significance of salvation and the substitutionary death of Jesus. The salvation of such a young person is resigned to the loving character of a wise and powerful God. Based on the infant death of King David's son, the Bible indicates that infants do go to Heaven when they die. It is reasonable to expect that which God did for David's son, He will do for all who die extremely young.

Let's consider the story of King David and his terminally ill infant son. David fasted and prayed asking God to spare his son, lying on his sickbed. David wore sackcloth and ashes and lamented over his son's illness. The King was unapproachable at this time by his servants for his grief was not hidden. Then, despite his prayers and petitions, David's son died which made his servants more fearful of being in the King's presence.

They reasoned that David's disposition would inevitably worsen now that his son had died. But the opposite happened. David cleaned himself up, got dressed, began to eat and, most importantly to worship God. The turnaround was so dramatic that all the servants did not know how to respond. King David then clarified his actions when he said, "But now that he is dead, why should I go on fasting? Can I bring him back again? I will go to him, but he will not return to me" (2 Samuel 12:23).

Both the story of Lazarus the poor beggar and the rich man, and that of David's son, speaks to the finality of death – there are no second chances. Would the rich man change his views and beliefs about Jesus if he could? His post-death change of heart indicates so as seen in his plea for his brothers when he asked Father Abraham to send them a sign. In his reasoning, no sign would be more powerful than to have them see Lazarus raised from the dead with a warning for them to repent.

The fact that the rich man remained in his place of torment calls attention to the seemingly impossible thing for a loving God to do; subject one of His prized creatures to an eternity of suffering. However, the rich man was a son of Abraham and undoubtedly had heard the teaching of Moses and the prophets' numerous times. He had turned a deaf ear to the message of salvation. Our eternal state is determined by the choices we make in this life, not the next.

As a very wealthy Jew, the rich man would have been taught that all material blessings were from God. He had neglected his duty to praise God and remember Him for those blessings (see Deuteronomy 8:10-20). Whether by personal observation or the report of a servant, one day the rich man realized that Lazarus no longer appeared begging at his gate. Lazarus had died. This gave the rich man an opportunity to reflect on his own mortality and to get right with God. Instead, he went on in life unconscious about the eventuality of his own death and the life choices he could have made.

Remember, in His great love, God is continually calling out to all people; "The Lord is not slow in keeping his promise, as some understand slowness. We would do well to remember that God is patient with you, not wanting anyone to perish, but everyone to come to repentance" (2 Peter 3:9).

It is interesting to note this rich man in Luke, Chapter 16, argued that, if someone from the dead brought a message back to the living, it would be so astonishing that people would repent and believe in God. Yet, in John, Chapter 11, we see that Jesus' friend Lazarus did come back to life, but for many, this did not lead to repentance. In fact, the religious leaders wanted to kill him and Jesus as well.

The Scriptures record nine people by name who were raised from the dead, and multitudes of others were raised when Jesus died (see Matthew 27:53). The most significant sign will have no effect on those who are determined not to believe. If we could believe by witnessing a supernatural sign, God would send plenty of them. Contextually, we have the Bible. If someone doesn't believe the Bible, by Jesus' own admission, they won't believe signs.

Read the word of Jesus recorded in Matthew 16:1-4: "The Pharisees and Sadducees came to Jesus and tested him by asking him to show them a sign from heaven. He replied, "When evening comes, you say, 'It will be fair weather, for the sky is red,' and in the morning, 'Today it will be stormy, for the sky is red and overcast.' You know how to interpret the appearance of the sky, but you cannot interpret the signs of the times. A wicked and adulterous generation looks for a sign, but none will be given it except the sign of Jonah."

Our contemporary society continues to look for mystical signs to anchor their faith, even when we have the most significant sign ever, the confirmed bodily resurrection of Jesus from the grave. As Jesus stated, we have the sign of Jonah, and no other sign will be given: "He (Jesus) answered, 'A wicked and adulterous generation asks for a sign! But none will be given it except the sign of the prophet Jonah. For as Jonah was three days and three nights in the belly of a huge fish, so the Son of Man will be three days and three nights in the heart of the earth'" (Matthew 12:39-40).

The resurrection of Jesus Christ from the grave is foundational to the Christian Faith. Former skeptics Josh McDowell (a lawyer) and Lee Strobel (an investigative journalist with the Chicago Tribune) set out independently to research and disprove the resurrection of Jesus Christ. In integrity, both men were convinced otherwise and documented their work in books called, *Evidence That Demands a Verdict,* and *The Case for Christ.* Both men concluded Jesus is the Christ. They are now Christian authors and evangelists for Jesus. I have recommended their books to people likewise searching for answers about Jesus. They are worth reading.[16]

Before leaving the rich man and Lazarus, I wish to probe deeper into the theology it expresses. Before Jesus rose from the grave and ushered in the New Testament era, priests would meet with God inside the Jewish Temple. Within the temple, there was a special room, called the Holy of Holies which was separated from the other areas by a thick curtain. Only the High Priest was permitted to go into the most sacred space – the Holy of Holies, and then only once per year. The curtain closing off the Holy of Holies symbolized that Man did not have direct access to God. It was only through Jesus' sacrifice in death that the curtain was torn in two, from top to bottom, symbolically opening man's access to God (see Matthew 27:51).

Scriptures tell us, that after Jesus died, he descended into the lower, earthly regions before ascending on high and taking many captives. The lower earthly regions (plural) were thought of as Sheol comprised into both Hades and Abraham's side. Those who had died in the Old Testament era were captives of the location they were consigned to as well as being captives of the sin which caused their death. The Apostle Paul addressed this: "When he ascended on high, he took many captives and gave gifts to his people. (What does 'he ascended' mean except that he also descended to the lower, earthly regions? He who descended is the very one who ascended higher than all the heavens, in order to fill the whole universe)" (Ephesians 4:8-10).

The Apostles Creed (of which there are various versions and nuances) declares the following statement of faith concerning Jesus Christ's death, burial and resurrection as well as an account of the time He spent between His death and His resurrection. In this version, we read:

"I believe in God, the Father Almighty, Creator of heaven and earth; and in Jesus Christ, His only Son, our Lord; who was conceived by the Holy Spirit, born of the

Virgin Mary, suffered under Pontius Pilate, was crucified, died and was buried; He descended into hell; the third day He arose again from the dead; He ascended into heaven, and sits at the right hand of God the Father Almighty; from there He will come to judge the living and the dead."

Though I had recited the Apostles creed when I attended church services in my childhood and read the passage in Ephesian 4:8-10 as an adult, I remained confused by the thought of Jesus descending into Hell and taking captives. However, after studying the subject of the life beyond, and specifically the story of these two dead people, it now makes sense.

Between his death and resurrection, Jesus paid a visit to Sheol, which is translated often as Hell in the New Testament. As previously noted, Sheol had two distinct sections; Abraham's Bosom (or Abraham's side), and Hades. He did this to release those who were held captive there, at Abraham's side. Paradise was soon to be opened, for Jesus promised the repentant thief who was crucified alongside Him, "Truly I tell you, today you will be with me in paradise" (Luke 23:43).

To be with Jesus would be to be with God. Once the curtain was torn in two, access to God was now fully available. Jesus came into the place known as Abraham's Bosom and returned with multitudes of Old Testament captives, including Lazarus, which He then ushered into Paradise.

CHAPTER 5 - PARADISE OR HEAVEN, HADES OR HELL?

"How well I have learned that there is no fence to sit on between heaven and hell. There is a deep, wide gulf, a chasm, and in that chasm is no place for any man."

Johnny Cash

Many biblical words are used when describing the next life; words like Paradise, Heaven, Hades, Hell, Gehenna, Sheol, and Abraham's Bosom. Other after-life places are noted in ancient civilizations and in various religious traditions, but it is beyond the scope of this book to discuss them all. Unfortunately, the different biblical words describing the afterlife add confusion to any discussion about the life beyond. Though similar, these words describe distinct places at distinct times. Some of these places no longer exist, some have yet to exist. Understanding these distinctions is imperative to understanding all that is to come after death.

I live in an area that is referred to in many ways. My home area can be called California, Northern California, Central Coast, The Bay Area, Monterey Bay, and Santa Cruz County to name just a few options. While all these names are generally accurate, there are distinctions among them. So it is with all the words in the Bible to describe Heaven and Hell. Here is a brief explanation of the differences.

Gehenna

According to Nelson's Bible Dictionary, Gehenna is the name of a valley outside of Jerusalem that was used as the public garbage dump. Trash, spoiled food, dead animals, and the bodies of the extremely poor and some criminals were dumped there. Everything disposable was burned by a fire that never died out, and everything not touched by the flame's heat was consumed by worms and maggots. It was a despised, unclean place that was avoided if possible. Jesus used it to illustrate the reality of everlasting torment; a picture of Hell. It was a real historical place, which exists today as the Valley of Hinnom, but it is no longer used as Jerusalem's city dump.

Sheol

Sheol was referred to as the place of the dead. Sheol is the Old Testament Hebrew word for "The Beyond," also known as the "common receptacle" for the dead. It is a term common in Old Testament times and is not as popular today. The equivalent word or thought today is "grave" which replaces the use of Sheol. It is essentially a substitute for the term death itself. To say that someone has gone to Sheol is the same as saying that they have died and gone to the grave. Though Sheol is not a word commonly used today, the concept it represents is still used.

Hades

Hades is a place of temporary torment where those destined for Hell are sent. You can think of Hades as an interim Hell from which there is no escape. Any who reject the work of Jesus on the cross for the forgiveness of their sins are sent there to await their final destination – eternal damnation. Many good and honorable people end up residing there since occupancy is not based on merit, but instead of the possession or not of faith in Jesus. Assignment to Hades belongs to those who, at death, are judged according to their lack of trust in Jesus, with their names not found in the Lamb's Book of Life (more to follow on this). The spirits of the dead who reside in Hades have some form of transitional body as they await their resurrected body at the last day. Hades still exists, though many today innocently prefer to call it Hell.

Note that the resurrection will take place for both the righteous and the unrighteous. Therefore, Hell does not presently exist. It will exist after the resurrection of the dead, at which time Hades will cease to exist. Those in Hell will have no contact with God or with other human beings.

Hell

Hell is the ultimate place of torment where all those in Hades will reside after the second coming of Christ and the resurrection of their bodies. They will no longer have transitional bodies but will have their original, yet immortal, body returned. Hades becomes Hell after the resurrection of the body as described in Daniel Chapter 12. "Multitudes who sleep in the dust of the earth will awake: some to everlasting life, others to shame and everlasting contempt" (Daniel 12:2).

Abraham's Bosom

Abraham's Bosom, or Abraham's side, was the Old Testament term used for those who died while still awaiting the Messiah. These were the righteous who believed by faith God's promise that a Savior was coming to redeem humankind. Since direct access to God was restricted for all humanity before Jesus died, those residing in Abraham's Bosom were not present with God but rather with the Father of their nation, Abraham. Upon the death and resurrection of Jesus, access to God was made available, the temple curtain was torn in two, symbolically giving access to God dwelling in the most Holy of Holies. Jesus visited the portion of Sheol known as Abraham's Bosom and took those righteous Believers waiting, with him into Paradise. Abraham's Bosom therefore no longer exists.

The Lamb's Book of Life

The Lamb's Book of Life is equally essential to understand. Biblically, Jesus is referred to as the Lamb of God who came to take away the sin of the world (see John 1:29). Whenever the Bible speaks of the Lamb as a person, this person is Jesus Christ. Furthermore, Jesus, the Lamb, maintains a documented record of all who believe in Him. This book is referred to the "Lamb's Book of Life" (see Revelation 13:8, 17:8, 20:15, 21:27). It is also known as The Book of Life.

Paradise

Today, when they die, Believers go to Paradise. These are the ones who have accepted Jesus and have their names written in the Lamb's Book of Life. Paradise is synonymous with the Garden of Eden, or Garden of Delight, in Genesis. Paradise is a Persian word that means a wooded park, an enclosed orchard or a garden with fruit trees. The Kings of Persia had exquisite gardens where entertainment and relaxation would occur. The garden was a place of exceptional favor, happiness, and delight.

The original Paradise, described in the book of Genesis, had many beautiful and fruit-bearing trees, including the tree of life, and the tree of the knowledge of good and evil (see Genesis 2:9). There was other seed-bearing vegetation, presumably grain crops, fruits, and vegetables for food (see Genesis 1:29). It was well watered ensuring lush vegetation and pasture land. In it, the first humans were placed along with all kinds of birds and land animals (see Genesis 2:19-20). When the first human beings, Adam and Eve, failed to obey God's directive not to eat the forbidden fruit, they sinned, and all of mankind was banished from Paradise. Yet God did not destroy it.

Paradise is mentioned three times in the New Testament. The first time it is used is in conjunction with a promise made by Jesus to the repentant thief who was dying next to him on his own cross. Jesus promised him, "...Truly I tell you, today you will be with me in *paradise*" (Luke 23:43).

The second time we find the word Paradise it is being spoken by the Apostle Paul. He writes, "And I know that this man—whether in the body or apart from the body I do not know, but God knows— was caught up to *paradise* and heard inexpressible things, things that no one is permitted to tell" (2 Corinthians 12:3-4).

The final occurrence of Paradise is found in Revelation, again associated with a promise. "Whoever has ears, let them hear what the Spirit says to the churches. To the one who is victorious, I will give the right to eat from the tree of life, which is in the *paradise* of God" (Revelation 2:7). Notice that Jesus, Paul, and John did not use the word, Heaven.

Paradise is different from Abraham's Bosom, and both are different from Heaven. Upon the death of Jesus, Abraham's Bosom has served its purpose, and it no longer exists, since all the Old Testament believers were taken from Abraham's Bosom and brought into Paradise.

Those of us who have accepted Jesus as the Savior, and die before His second coming, will join the redeemed captives Jesus brought from Sheol in Paradise. In Paradise, we will dwell with God for eternity. In time, both Hades and Paradise will no longer exist as both will be replaced by Hell and Heaven. One who dies before the second coming of Christ will reside first in Paradise and then in Heaven, or in Hades and then in Hell. Again, our destination is determined in this life and confirmed in the next. "Nothing impure will ever enter it (Heaven), nor will anyone who does what is shameful or deceitful, but only those whose names are written in the Lamb's Book of Life" (Revelation 21:27).

Despite our inability to physically see it, Paradise remains a present reality. We do not know where Paradise is physically located today. We can speculate that it is in a different part of the universe, or it may be hidden from our eyes in an unknown spiritual and physical dimension here on Earth. I am reminded of the servant of Elisha who was paralyzed with fear until Elisha asked God to give his servant a glimpse of the invisible realm. "Then the Lord opened the servant's eyes, and he looked and saw the hills full of horses and chariots of fire all around Elisha" (2 Kings 6:17). Who knows? Paradise may be right here in our own back yard.

Heaven

Paradise and Heaven both exist today. As mentioned in the Lord's Prayer, God the Father dwells in the present Heaven (see Matthew 6:9). Paradise is the current place believers go to when they die. Our future home is Heaven where we will live with God in our resurrected bodies.

Paradise is "up there" somewhere while the future Heaven will be "down here" once God delivers on His promise to make a New Heaven and a New Earth (see 2 Peter 3:13). God's ultimate plan is not to take us up to live in a realm designed for Him, but rather to come down and live with us in the realm made for us – a perfected, recreated place for us. A home without weeds, pollution, corruption, and crime. More importantly, a place without sin, death, sorrow, separation, fear or pain.

The New Heaven will be very familiar to us, as it will be located on the New (refreshed) Earth. We do not know with certainty if the New Earth is comprised of renewed elements or if it is entirely new. We are familiar with this Earth and the idea that God calls its renewal the "New Earth" leads us to imagine familiar features. We know mountains, rivers, and oceans, yet we don't know unpolluted mountains, rivers, and oceans. I can picture beautiful cities, but I can't picture cities without crime and corruption. Dwelling places that will need no doors, windows that need no locks. What awaits the believer, though familiar, will be distinct enough to render it nearly unbelievable. As declared in the Lord's Prayer, "Your kingdom come, your will be done on earth as in Heaven" (Matthew 6:10).

Chapter 6 - Hell No

"All your life an attainable ecstasy has hovered just beyond the grasp of your consciousness. The day is coming when you will wake to find, beyond all hope, that you have attained it, or else, that it was in your reach and you have lost it forever."

CS Lewis

A comprehensive study of the Bible reveals that Jesus is the one who says more about Hell than anyone else. He describes it as a literal place, in extremely graphic terms. He points out that it includes raging fires, the worm that doesn't die, darkness, being thrown outside, weeping and the gnashing of teeth. Jesus' description consists of both external torment (fire) and internal torment (worms). His teaching is summarized in these four sobering points:

1. <u>Hell as a Place of Torment</u>

Hell will be a place of torment including both emotional and physical pain. Jesus' description is frightening: "The Son of Man will send out his angels, and they will weed out of his kingdom everything that causes sin and all who do evil. They will throw them into the blazing furnace, where there will be weeping and gnashing of teeth" (Matthew 13:41-42).

Weeping is a sign of emotional agony, sorrow, and grief. I relate this to the morning I received a call from one of my best friends informing me that his 26-year-old son became ill and died suddenly and unexpectantly. My heart broke for my friend and his wife, and all I could do was weep. I knew no other way to express my agony, sorrow, and grief.

On the other hand, the gnashing of teeth is a sign of physical agony. I've broken several bones, suffered from internal bleeding, and have been hospitalized six times. The pain I experienced resulted in the gritting of my teeth and deep groans. Jesus warns us that this torment, magnified many times over, waits for those who reject him. Worse, there is no indication that one will ever get over this emotional and physical agony. It will last forever.

2. **Hell will be Eternal**

As hard as this is to accept, Hell will be everlasting. Referring to the bodily resurrection of the dead, Daniel stated, "Multitudes who sleep in the dust of the earth will awake: some to everlasting life, others to shame and everlasting contempt" (Daniel 12:2).

The Hebrew word *olam*, which translates as everlasting in English, was significantly chosen to describe both life and contempt. *Olam* means "beyond the vanishing point," or "time out of mind." Everlasting looks so far into the future that when your mind reaches the extent of how futuristic it can be, there is still unimaginable time beyond that point.

Jesus speaks of everlasting by referring to undying worms and unquenched fire, "And if your eye causes you to stumble, pluck it out. It is better for you to enter the kingdom of God with one eye than to have two eyes and be thrown into hell, where 'the worms that eat them do not die, and the fire is not quenched'" (Mark 9:47-48).

Here, Jesus was apparently referring to Gehenna, Jerusalem's city garbage dump. The endless piles of trash would be thrown into this valley where a fire would consume everything combustible (including human flesh). The worm would eat away at all residual flesh which did not burn, along with the other rotting material.

I am reminded of the time I was hiking in the forest and came across a deer that had recently died. It was covered with thousands of maggots, and its smell was unlike any rotten smell I had ever experienced. It was a disgusting sight to behold and an example Jesus selected to communicate the appalling reality of Hell. Jesus used the most graphic of terms to make sure His warning was clear.

3. <u>Hell will Encompass Eternal Punishment</u>

Hell will be a place of eternal punishment. It is the antithesis of Heaven. Heaven will be a place of wonder, delight, happiness, blessedness, and joy eternal. Heaven will include everything that is good. We will see God face-to-face and be in His presence forever. Perfection, ecstasy, fulfillment, and purpose will define our existence. Hell will be the complete opposite.

Jesus taught us that eternal life would be for those headed to Heaven, as well as for those who are headed to Hell. "Then they will go away to eternal punishment, but the righteous to eternal life" (Matthew 25:46). Those who think God would never consign anyone to an eternal place of torment, fail to recognize that Jesus never presented such an option. Jesus used the same word eternal to describe both punishment and life. According to Jesus, we cannot believe in eternal life without believing in eternal punishment. By His choice of words, Jesus never gave us that option.

4. Hell is the Opposite of Heaven

We rightfully think of Heaven as a place of everlasting bliss where all pain, suffering, crying, tears, disease, and death will no longer be found. All will be good, relationships will be fantastic, motives will be pure, and trust will be given.

We look forward to Heaven where we will be fully known, thoroughly loved, and know Christ fully (see 1 Corinthians 13:12). We will see Him and be like Him, transformed with nothing coming between us; no shadows and no doubts. To know His incredible mind, to behold Him and see His beauty, like a prism split into millions of fragments, each one cause us to see Him and be able to worship Him in a new way. The longing of every human heart is to know Him, and that deep longing can only be filled by Him. We will only know this relationship in Heaven, but we can be thankful now for the glimpses he gives us.

But, as stated earlier, Hell is just the opposite. By logical necessity, because God is the source of all good, and Hell is the absence of God, Hell must also be the absence of all good, including light and companionship.

Especially painful will be the absence of community, camaraderie, and friendship. Perhaps you have heard the saying, "Misery loves company." In Hell, there will be nothing to love and no one to help. No one to come alongside and commiserate. Unlike the imaginings of some, Hell will not be the place to booze it up and party. Hell is not the place where all the cool people go. Our understanding of Hell has been warped by people who have represented God, without knowing God. False perceptions of Hell have been embraced without considering what the Son of God had to say about it.

The best parties I have gone to are wedding receptions. People are happy, and food and drink are plentiful. Everyone is in a good mood. No other party compares to that of a wedding celebration. Therefore, appropriately, the first event in Heaven, after the resurrection of our bodies, will be the wedding feast of Christ and His bride, the Church. If you want to party, you need to end up in Heaven – AND you are invited.

In rebuking some religious leaders who falsely thought they were a part of God's family, Jesus said of them, "But the subjects of the kingdom (those who think they are close to God but actually far away) will be thrown outside, into the darkness, where there will be weeping and gnashing of teeth" (Matthew 8:12).

Unfortunately, many associate their religious deeds – church attendance, giving, serving, reading their Bible, praying and the such as the "pass" needed to avoid Hell. Jesus is not interested in our good works, in fact, His Word refers to them as filthy rags. "All of us have become like one who is unclean, and all our righteous acts are like filthy rags" (Isaiah 64:6).

Jesus attacked the self-righteousness of the religious leaders of his day. Faith is not a garment worn on the outside, it is a change of heart on the inside; something accomplished only by the grace of God.

We often associate light with fire, but in this case, we are only offered darkness – utter darkness. Years ago, while on vacation in Central Oregon, my wife and I paid an entrance fee to take our children into an underground cave. It was a sweltering day with temperatures nearing 100 degrees, but 25 feet underground the temperature dropped to about 40 degrees. We were told that the ancient Native American Indians used caves as a natural refrigerator to keep food from perishing. We chose to walk to the end of the cave until we could only crawl on our bellies to proceed further. As we came to the end of how far we could travel, I suggested we turn off our flashlights.

That was a mistake. The darkness was terrifying, and unlike any other darkness, I had ever experienced. Even in a "dark" room, our eyes eventually adjust to whatever little ambient light is present. But the eternal darkness of Hell will be like the utter darkness of that cave.

From my earliest years, living in the Western culture, I have heard that I can accomplish anything, and therefore I should never let anyone get in the way of my goals. This social construct is seen through W.I. Thomas's important Thomas Theorem which states, "If men define situations as real, they are real in their consequences" (Thomas and Thomas 1928).[17] This theorem proposes that objective reality is not as important as a person's subjective construction of reality in determining behavior. And behavior determines outcomes.

The result is an increasing level of confusion in our society and in our understanding of life after death. We naively think that if there is no Hell (subjectively), then there is no Hell (objectively). If all go to Heaven (subjectively), then all go to Heaven (objectively). If we die and our spirits merge into one constant cosmic force (subjectively), then that is what will happen (objectively). Collectively we are moving further and further away from objective reality.

Jesus told the parable of the wise and foolish builders indicating we have the freedom to determine the underpinnings of our reality. He taught this as an invitation to build our belief system on the objective truth of His teaching (see Matthew 7:24-27).

Considering what the Christian Bible has to say about the afterlife is a rational pursuit, especially when it comes to its teaching on Hell. Yes, the Bible does teach that there is a literal place of eternal torment called Hell. Those who believe they will never go there, reason that they are basically good; they embody more good than evil and whose good deeds outnumber the bad. We hold onto such a merit-based philosophy because we want it to be true. We falsely assume that God grades on a curve and all that we are required to do is to get a passing grade. In embracing this philosophy, we increasingly deny our need for a savior.

I live on the central coast of California next to the Pacific Ocean. There are many ocean swimmers here, including some who can swim the 40 miles distance between the city of Santa Cruz and the city of Monterey – the breadth of the Monterey Bay. I would be fortunate to cover one hundred yards before I sank! I think we would all agree, that however good a swimmer one is, no one is good enough to swim 2,336 miles from Santa Cruz to Hawaii.

To think that we can merit our way into Heaven is analogous to believing that we can swim our way to Hawaii. We fail to understand the reality, power, and magnitude of sin – as it is the only universal thing that can keep us out of Heaven. We may not want to hear this, but Hell is our default destination. If I want to get to Hawaii, I need help getting there. If I want to get to Heaven, I also need help getting there; I cannot get there on my own, that is why Jesus, and his work on the cross, is so cherished in my heart.

Sin is easily misunderstood. The word "sin" has its origin as an archer's term. It simply means to miss the target. That no matter how skilled or strong one is in releasing an arrow, it always comes up short. The target here is the righteousness of God, and we all fall short. The Scriptures declare, "For all have sinned and fall short of the glory of God" (Romans 3:23). Again, we read in the Bible, "Indeed, there is no one on earth who is righteous, no one who does what is right and never sins" (Ecclesiastes 7:20).

In our arrogance, we are comfortable defining degrees of sin, and we take false hope in thinking that our minor lies, occasional gossip and petty envy are not in the same class as murder, rape, sexual immorality and the like. How wrong we are. All sin is detestable to God. Knowing how God sees sin can help us from judging others' sins; we have our own sin to deal with.

Jesus died to take away the sin of the world. The sin that will keep us out of Heaven is the sin of rejecting Jesus. Consider the prophet Habakkuk who declares about God, "Your eyes are too pure to look on evil; you cannot tolerate wrongdoing" (Habakkuk 1:13).

Getting to Heaven without Jesus washing away your sin is impossible. Again, we must understand that without intervention, without a Savior, Hell is our default destination.

If it were possible to enter Heaven with sin in our hearts, then it would take no time at all for Heaven to become much like Earth. In short order, it would begin to swell with people of pride, envy, gossip, slandering, lies, greed, sexual immorality, impurity, debauchery, idolatry, witchcraft, hatred, selfish ambition and the like. But it is not possible to enter Heaven with such sin; God has previously warned us, "...that those who live like this will not inherit the kingdom of God" (Galatians 5:19-21).

It is said of Heaven, "Nothing impure will ever enter it, nor will anyone who does what is shameful or deceitful, but only those whose names are written in the Lamb's book of life" (Revelation 21:27).

As we have discussed, sin demands a payment be made. Therefore, Jesus took on the punishment that was due us, so that we could be made spotless in his sight. Consider the severity of this warning given by the Apostle Paul, "He will punish those who do not know God and do not obey the Gospel of our Lord Jesus. They will be punished with everlasting destruction and shut out from the presence of the Lord and from the glory of his might" (2 Thessalonians 1:8-9).

Do I have your attention? Notice that Paul was not saying it is those who do not know *of* God who will go to Hell, but rather those who do not *know* God will be the ones shut out from the presence of the Lord. To *know* God in this context is to *know* God *experientially*. It is the idea of having a relationship with God through which we know His character, His love, and His thoughts toward us.

For some, this may be the most difficult of all the sections to read. Some readers may have recently lost a loving friend or family member to death and feel confident that they are in heaven – despite what Jesus may have taught. After all, the loved one they knew was a good person.

Even the thought of the potential of Hell is difficult, primarily if your loved one was indeed a great, kind and loving person. Unfortunately, those qualities are not Heaven's entrance requirements. The picture Jesus paints is not a pretty one; quite the opposite – it is terrifying!

The consolation I offer is the hope that at one time in your loved one's life, he or she decided to make Jesus their Lord and Savior. Perhaps this happened when the person was a young child or in the moments before death. Maybe the decision made never developed into a lifetime of worshipping Jesus. What we do with Jesus in our lives is a separate subject altogether, and I encourage you to find ways to investigate this further.

The mention of the eternal life Jesus offers to us is stated as a present, active, indicative verb. That is, the tense is present (describing action taking place now), the voice is active (meaning that the verb's subject is acting and not being acted upon), and the mood is indicative (which demonstrates true reality). Jesus said, "Very truly I tell you, whoever hears my word and believes him who sent me has eternal life and will not be judged but has crossed over from death to life" (John 5:24).

Once eternal life is possessed, it cannot be lost. I urge all of us to hang onto the possibility that at one time our dear one did make a profession of faith in Christ. Do not let the hint of them possibly being in Hell, keep us from trusting in Jesus, and securing our own future away from there.

When our life is evaluated, our faith will be shown for what it is. The Scriptures declare that people will go to heaven based on their faith in Christ even though they have nothing else to show for their faith (see 1 Corinthians 3:10-15). It may look like they narrowly escaped the flames of Hell.

If we would grasp the agony, loneliness and pure dread of Hell we would *never* attempt to consign someone there through our words – not even our worst enemy. Those who end up in Hell will feel small, insignificant, without companionship, purpose, vision, or accomplishment. One could speculate that there is a grand conspiracy, led by Satan, to get all humans to fearlessly reject Jesus and his offer of eternal life in Heaven. And to rejecting Him without a second thought. That is a premise this book challenges.

At the end of 2018, the people of the United States were captivated by the proceedings of the US Senate hearings regarding the appointment of Judge Kavanaugh to the US Supreme Court. The allegations of sexual misconduct which surfaced from Dr. Ford polarized our nation. I have no comment on his guilt or the possible innocence of his alleged indiscretions as a teenager, but the testimony from both sides stirred my heart to recount some of my teen years. The Lord woke me up in the middle of a Monday night, and I began recalling not just accusations, but actual events that I participated in when I was a teenager.

I was overcome with shame, guilt, and regret for my wild and careless, self-centered lifestyle. I was a sinner of the worst kind and yet at the time of my youth I distinctively remember thinking that I was a "good person." I attended church, I was a good student, a good son, a good worker, and in my mind, my good outweighed the bad. How wrong I was! Had I died at the time, I would have been sent to Hell for eternity, for I had never accepted the death Jesus died as a substitute for my sins.

I had never said *"Hell No"* and repented of my sin (my separation) with my God who loves me. Now just the thought of separation and knowing that I was headed to Hell is overwhelmingly despairing to me. Simultaneously, I have tremendous gratitude for the love my Savior showed me.

Praise God, I was not left in that state forever. I believe God had tried relentlessly to show me His love and had pursued a friendship with me the first thirty years of my life, *despite my resistance*. At the age of thirty, I allowed His love to break through. I repented of my sins and turned 180 degrees into the arms of Jesus. I had thought that I was far from him, but when I turned, he was right there.

Jesus's grace has healed me and repaired my brokenness. In the second half of my life, I am experiencing peace, joy, and love at levels I had only imagined. I have the assurance that when I die, I will not go to Hell. I will be ushered into the presence of God and enter Heaven. This is not because I deserve Heaven – I don't. I have acknowledged the reality of Hell and what Jesus accomplished on the cross for the forgiveness of my sins.

Forgiveness represents one of God's greatest gifts. In His great love, he does not give us what we deserve. This is called Mercy. Instead, he gives us what we do not deserve. This is called Grace.

I would like to address the question of whether someone who lacks knowledge of Jesus goes to Hell. The Bible does not give us a direct answer to that question. The Bible only addresses those who have heard of the salvation offered by Jesus; therefore, we need to build our response by whatever supporting evidence provided by the Bible.

The Bible informs us that the Lord is a God of justice (see Isaiah 30:18). God is gracious, slow to anger, abounding in love and faithfulness (see Exodus 34:6), and that the Judge of all the earth will do right (see Genesis 18:25). We can lean on God's character and speculate that whatever might happen to the one who has never heard of Jesus, that God will treat that person according to His character. But we also know that those who truly seek after God will find Him (see Matthew 7:7).

In his book, *Miraculous Movements* author Jerry Trousdale explains how hundreds of thousands of Muslims are falling in love with Jesus. Many of these people live in remote areas without access to the Bible. Many have stories of dreams of Jesus coming to visit them because of their genuine desire to know God.

Jesus desires to be known. We are told that "God's invisible qualities—his eternal power and divine nature—have been clearly seen, being understood from what has been made, so that people are without excuse" (Romans 1:20).

We are even told, "The heavens declare the glory of God; the skies proclaim the work of his hands. Day after day they pour forth speech; night after night they reveal knowledge" (Psalm 19:1-2).

This question of asking about the fate of those without knowledge of Jesus is an academic one. What is most important is that we realize and accept that God desires that all people be reconciled unto Him, and the Church must make Him known. We have a message to share.

Many people want to go to Heaven, and many people think they are going to Heaven. However, *Hell No* must come before *Heaven Yes*! To say no to Hell, one must believe what Jesus teaches about it. To say "yes" to Heaven, we must "say" yes to Jesus.

CHAPTER 7 - HEAVEN YES

"The good news is there is nothing we can do that is bad enough to keep us out of Heaven; the bad news is there is nothing we can do good enough to get us into Heaven."

Zig Ziglar

To the one who remains apart from Jesus, death is your greatest enemy. Death is coming, and there is nothing you can do to stop it. No one has defeated death _except_ Jesus Christ. With the cold calculated certainty of the Roman military, experts at putting people to death, Jesus was crucified and laid to rest in a guarded tomb. On the third day, He rose from the grave thus defeating death. He did this by defeating death's fundamental cause, namely the penalty of sin which was forgiven at the cross. The one who receives Jesus no longer needs to fear death. Death is no longer the enemy.

In ancient times it was common for people to enter into covenants with each other. Covenants were binding oaths, made between two people, that defined their relationship going forward. According to Nelson's Bible Dictionary, "A covenant, in the biblical sense, implies much more than a contract or simple agreement. A contract always has an end date, while a covenant is a permanent arrangement. Another difference is that a contract generally involves only one part of a person, such as a skill, while a covenant covers a person's total being."

It was common for the two parties of a covenant to exchange weapons as a symbol that they would vow to fight each other's enemies from that point forward. They would also agree to protect each other. Israel's King David and his good friend Jonathan entered such a covenant and weapons were exchanged (see 1 Samuel 18:3-4). On numerous occasions, Jonathan protected David from his enemy, who happened to be Jonathan's father, Saul.[18] In the end, Saul became his son Jonathan's enemy as well.[19]

Satan is not the enemy of humanity. The enemy of humanity is death. Jesus' enemy is Satan. The moment you confess belief in Jesus these enemies are exchanged. Jesus takes on our enemy death and defeats it. Death holds no power over the soul believing in Jesus. But, since we are joined with Christ, Satan becomes our new enemy. We become a threat to his rule and dominion. Jesus fights our enemy for us. Ultimate victory belongs to Jesus, and in the end, after the resurrection of the dead, Satan will be consigned forever to the burning lake of fire, also known as Hell (see Revelation 20:14).

I love to cook and bake as a hobby. When we invite people to our home for dinner, I am the one who does the cooking. In my younger years, I had just enough restaurant experience to pick up a love for the kitchen.

As I carefully write this book, I feel like I am creating a multi-layered cake. The arguments are presented layer on layer, with repetition, to build a Biblical perspective of the life beyond.

We have learned that at death our body returns to dust, and our spirit returns to God. Our faith is evaluated and sealed. There is no further chance to modify it. If we chose against Jesus Christ in life, in death our choice is made absolute. There is no mention in the Bible of any time delay between death on Earth and continued life in the next realm. A person dead in Christ is not a lost person; rather that person is separated from us, and their body, yet fully alive, now in the presence of God. That is why Paul can confidently state, "Brothers and sisters, we do not want you to be uninformed about those who sleep in death, so that you do not grieve like the rest of mankind, who have no hope" (1 Thessalonians 4:13).

This truth led famed Pastor, Evangelist, and Theologian D.L. Moody to declare, "Someday you will read in the newspaper that I am dead. Don't believe it for a moment. I will be more alive than ever before."[20] The same thing can be said of us. Paul stated this truth using other words when he wrote, "I am torn between the two: I desire to depart and be with Christ, which is better by far; but it is more necessary for you that I remain in the body" (Philippians 1:23-24).

Only two options are given; to be alive here on Earth, or to be alive in the next realm. In other words, there is direct continuity from one life to the next.

As we consider our continuity, however, is it just the spirit that continues and if so, what is made of our bodies? The spirit's departure from the body ends our existence on Earth. Until, if we have accepted Christ's invitation, we join him on the New Earth. The physical part of us "sleeps" until the resurrection, while the spiritual part (for the believer in Jesus) relocates to a conscious existence in Paradise. Our bodily resurrection will come, but it is delayed until the culmination of time when Jesus will come a second time. Daniel revealed, "Multitudes who sleep in the dust of the earth will awake: some to everlasting life, others to shame and everlasting contempt" (Daniel 12:2).

There is a fascinating report the Apostle John gave us recording a scene in Paradise. He writes, "When he opened the fifth seal, I saw under the altar the souls of those who had been slain because of the word of God and the testimony they had maintained. They called out in a loud voice, 'How long, Sovereign Lord, holy and true, until you judge the inhabitants of the earth and avenge our blood?' Then each of them was given a white robe, and they were told to wait a little longer, until the full number of their fellow servants, their brothers and sisters, were killed just as they had been" (Revelation 6:9-11).

It appears that while we wait for our physical bodies to be resurrected, we are given some type of transitional body. Consider what John the Revelator saw. It takes vocal cords to call out in a loud voice. It takes a body to be clothed in a robe. This does not describe a spiritual existence only.

Furthermore, as we saw presented in the story of two dead people (Chapter 5), the rich man had a tongue and a thirst he wished to satisfy with a drop of water. Lazarus also had a finger to dip into the water. They both had eyes to see and ears to hear. They could reason and recognize, indicating they had mental capacity (brains).

The Apostle John had a body when he visited heaven for, he grasped, held, ate, and tasted things there. "So I went to the angel and asked him to give me the little scroll. He said to me, 'Take it and eat it. It will turn your stomach sour, but 'in your mouth it will be as sweet as honey.' I took the little scroll from the angel's hand and ate it. It tasted as sweet as honey in my mouth, but when I had eaten it, my stomach turned sour" (Revelation 10:9-10).

When caught up to the third Heaven, Paul the Apostle was unsure if he had a body or not. "I know a man in Christ who fourteen years ago was caught up to the third heaven. Whether it was in the body or out of the body I do not know—God knows. And I know that this man—whether in the body or apart from the body I do not know, but God knows..." (2 Corinthians 12:2-3). His uncertainty over possessing a body may be that the transitional body we will receive is distinctively different from our present bodies of flesh and blood.

Another thought about transitional bodies and the continuity of life: we have no record anywhere in the

Bible that at any time humankind existed without both a body and a spirit. Unlike God and the angels, who are spirits, human beings are by nature both spiritual and physical. "God is spirit, and his worshipers must worship in the Spirit and in truth" (John 4:24). "Are not all angels ministering spirits sent to serve those who will inherit salvation?" (Hebrews 1:14).

From the beginning, the essence of human beings is both spirit and body. "Then the Lord God formed a man from the dust of the ground and breathed into his nostrils the breath of life, and the man became a living being" (Genesis 2:7).

A further point is that we will remain fully conscious at death as explained by the Apostle Paul. Nearing the end of his life, Paul was imprisoned in Rome, and he was torn between living and dying as he told, "For to me, to live is Christ and to die is gain. If I am to go on living in the body, this will mean fruitful labor for me. Yet what shall I choose? I do not know! I am torn between the two: I desire to depart and be with Christ, which is better by far; but it is more necessary for you that I remain in the body" (Philippians 1:21-24). This passage indicates that after we take our last breath here on Earth, our very next breath will be in the presence of God. Paul mentions no other alternative. Death does not remove from us life; it only transforms our life.

Can you see that Paul, the one who wrote thirteen books of the New Testament, expressed extreme confidence in knowing that at his death he would immediately be ushered into the presence of God? He taught a continuity of awareness and consciousness from this life to the next – his heart never skipping a beat, his lungs never lacking a breath.

Paul included this teaching to the church in Corinth in the writing of his second letter when he declared, "Therefore we are always confident and know that as long as we are at home in the body we are away from the Lord. For we live by faith, not by sight. We are confident, I say, and would prefer to be away from the body and at home with the Lord" (2 Corinthians 5:6-8). The thought is repeated that such a thing as soul-sleep is not considered an option.

There are verses in the Bible that speak of death as one who "sleeps in death" (1 Thessalonians 4:13). This language is used to describe a body that has died, for a dead person may look like they are sleeping, even though they are not breathing. The reason the thought of sleeping was applied to a person who had died is that it accurately illustrates the reality of the resurrection of the body at a future date. People wake up from sleep. So too our bodies will wake up from the dead (from the dust) and be resurrected in the future.

Jesus entered a village once and was met by a man named Jairus, a synagogue leader. His twelve-year-old daughter was dying, and Jairus was trying his best to reach Jesus before she died so that he might heal her. Jairus had lost hope after his daughter died. He was gathered with his family and friends, at his house, crying and wailing loudly as they collectively grieved. However, before Jesus raised her from the dead, He made a startling statement when he said, "The child is not dead but asleep. However, they laughed at him" (Mark 5:39). This story, told in three of the four Gospels, shows us that only the body sleeps, but one day it will be resurrected.

When we read in the Bible, mention of the dead who are asleep, remember that what is being taught is the body "sleeping" as it awaits its resurrection. The Apostle Paul understood this concept when he explained the Gospel message. As he spoke of the resurrection of Jesus, he noted that the resurrected Jesus had appeared to more than five hundred people thirty years earlier though by then some of those eyewitnesses had died. Consider Paul's word's, "After that, he appeared to more than five hundred of the brothers and sisters at the same time, most of whom are still living, though some have fallen asleep" (1 Corinthians 15:6).

The question of who is saved is not determined in Heaven but in this present life here on Earth. In Heaven, we receive the final confirmation of who is in and who is out. This is revealed by the inclusion, or exclusion, in the Lamb's Book of Life. To enter Heaven, we must be as pure as God himself. The Apostle John revealed, "Nothing impure will ever enter it (Heaven), nor will anyone who does what is shameful or deceitful, but only those whose names are written in the Lamb's book of life" (Revelation 21:27).

Remember it is Jesus who is the Lamb of God, the only one who can purify us from our sins and give us any hope at all of being with Him in Heaven.

The Lamb's Book of Life is mentioned by the Old Testament Prophet Daniel, "... everyone whose name is found written in the Book—will be delivered" (Daniel 12:1). The Book of Life is referred to by the Apostle Paul as he spoke of his partners in ministry. "Yes, and I ask you, my true companion, help these women since they have contended at my side in the cause of the Gospel, along with Clement and the rest of my co-workers, whose names are in the Book of Life" (Philippians 4:3).

Be assured that in this life, before our hour of death, we want our name to be written into the Book of Life. This is a decision we should make without delay.

Jesus went to extraordinary lengths to save us from an eternity separated from Him, to bring us to an eternity with Him. Jesus took on our sin, and paid the penalty meant for us. He endured "excruciating" pain. In fact, the very word excruciating is derived from the pain of being nailed to a cross; literally "out of the cross" pain. If you have not done so already, why not accept Jesus right now? You can do so by inviting Jesus into your life through a simple prayer such as this:

Dear God, I admit that I am a sinner. My sin deserves to be punished. I accept the fact that you went to the cross, took on my sin, and died in my place. I believe that you were buried and that you rose from the grave three days later. You have defeated sin and death – specifically my sin and my death. I invite you to take over my life, and from now on I will call upon you as my Savior and follow you as my Lord. In Jesus' name, Amen!

CHAPTER 8 - THE CURSE REVERSED

"Every blessing ignored becomes a curse."

Paulo Coelho

All we have ever known or experienced in life has been lived under the curse of sin. We are not strangers to hardship, loneliness, sickness, decay, pollution, corruption, loss and other terms that convey evidence of a broken and damaged world. Since Adam and Eve disobeyed God and committed their original sin in the garden of Eden, the consequences have been disastrous not only on human life but on all of creation.

It is God's intent that mankind lives through three distinct eras. The period before the Curse was the first era. The Bible devotes two Chapters, Genesis Chapters 1 and 2, to this era. The second era, the one we know presently, is living under the Curse. This covers most of the Bible. The final age, which will be after the Curse is lifted, is represented in the last two Chapters of the Bible, Revelation Chapters 21 and 22.

In the first era, God created a pristine, flawless world for humankind to dwell in, explore, and manage. After each day of creation, God proclaimed that what He had made "was good." On the final day of creation, He announced all that He had made was "very good." Before the Curse, humanity had a relationship with God, sin was unknown, and there was no shame or death. Food and water were plentiful, work was meaningful, and relationships were intimate. This describes the essence of Paradise we have lost. Heaven was on Earth. Someday this will be true once again.

In the beginning, before the Curse of mankind, there was no death for sin had yet entered the world. There was dominion given to humanity over all of creation because the perfect man could rule an ideal creation. God's blessing was poured out on all of creation and the responsibility given honored and dignified mankind. A study of Genesis Chapters 1 and 2 invites our imagination to consider what it must have been like and to inspire us to return to a time such as that.

Consider that food and water were readily available with a minimum of labor. Time was plentiful to pursue creative aesthetic ideas. Today we have things we want to pursue, but we often don't have the time to follow through. Not so in the Garden of Eden. The work man was given to do was done with sheer pleasure. How many of us can say that of our jobs today?

I wonder if the widespread desire for early retirement is an indicator of our hunger to pursue our hobbies for the sheer enjoyment of it; something connecting our hearts to what was lost by the Curse? The intelligence granted to man allowed him to please and glorify God by continually learning and developing new skills and abilities.

In the Garden of Eden man was given only one prohibition: do not eat of the fruit of the tree of the knowledge of good and evil. Easy enough, right? Wrong! All that our ancestors had to do was to deny themselves of this one thing. Everything else in all of creation was available to them. God placed before them (and us today) a choice to demonstrate love and obedience. The decision results in life or death. God's prohibition came with a clear warning; if they were to eat of the fruit, they would surely die.

The failure of Adam and Eve ushered in the forewarned Curse, recorded for us in these foreboding words, "To Adam he said, 'Because you listened to your wife and ate fruit from the tree about which I commanded you, 'You must not eat from it,' 'Cursed is the ground because of you; through painful toil you will eat food from it all the days of your life'" (Genesis 3:17).

We have all suffered from the effects of the Curse. The manifestation of sin is vividly expressed by the writer of the book of Galatians: "The acts of the flesh are obvious: sexual immorality, impurity, and debauchery; idolatry and witchcraft; hatred, discord, jealousy, fits of rage, selfish ambition, dissensions, factions and envy; drunkenness, orgies, and the like. I warn you, as I did before, that those who live like this will not inherit the kingdom of God" (Galatians 5:19-21). Fortunately, those in Heaven will not have to contend with such evil, because those who live like this and don't turn to Jesus, will be barred from entering.

To repeat, everything we have experienced in this life has been under the great Curse. How many of us have had our lives impacted by the ugliness of man? How many have suffered because of strife, hatred, envy, anger, verbal abuse, divorce, physical abuse, addiction, betrayal and the like?

I find it fascinating how adept we humans can be at shifting blame. It is commonly viewed that if God is so good, powerful and knowing, He could easily solve every problem, but because issues remain, He must be at fault. Or at minimum, He must not be as good, powerful and knowing as He claims to be. We have placed the blame for man's condition on God. This is one of the greatest injustices; perhaps second only to the sinless Son of God dying for our sins.

When first reading of the dietary restriction placed on Adam and Eve, it appears as though God's initial warning of certain death never happened. "And the Lord God commanded the man, 'You are free to eat from any tree in the garden; but you must not eat from the tree of the knowledge of good and evil, for when you eat from it you will certainly die'" (Genesis 2:17).

Adam and Eve disobeyed God and ate the forbidden fruit, but they did not die; at least not immediately. Once they tasted the fruit and allowed its juices to flow down their throats and death never came, their spiritual eyes were opened, and they realized a previously unknown separation in their relationship with God. None of this surprised an all-knowing God.

I believe God allowed them to continue living as His first act of grace toward humankind. He could have ended humanity right then and there. But the Lord did not. God decided that to live under the Curse, with a chance at redemption, would be better than not living at all.

He has given us the chance to live, the opportunity to choose Him, and the possibility of returning to a recreated Earth. God is not to blame. Here is the hope we hang onto. "No longer will there be any curse. The throne of God and of the Lamb will be in the city, and his servants will serve him" (Revelation 22:3).

The Curse is real, but the Curse is temporary. The Bible contains no greater promise, it holds out no greater hope, than informing us that the day is coming when no longer will there be any Curse.

Jesus tasted the bitterness of the Curse when His good friend Lazarus died. Had the Curse never entered the world, His friend would never have died. Jesus witnessed the pain and suffering Lazarus' death caused to his sisters, Mary and Martha, and those close to their family. Jesus saw firsthand what the Curse had done to all that He proclaimed to be good, and because Jesus became flesh, He experienced the effects of the Curse. The weeping and wailing after Lazarus was placed in the grave were a cold reminder of the Curse. Though Jesus did call Lazarus forth from the grave, before He did, He broke down in tears. The separation caused by death was too much for even Jesus to accept. In the shortest of all verses, "Jesus wept" (John 11:35).

But more than taste the Curse, Jesus became the Curse for us. As the Scriptures state, "Cursed is everyone who is hung on a pole" (Galatians 3:13). Jesus became sin as he took on the sin of every one of us. "God made him who had no sin to be sin for us, so that in him we might become the righteousness of God" (2 Corinthians 5:21). What a gift. Make a note of the contrast. The work of the devil (Satan) is sin, while the work of Jesus is righteousness, life, forgiveness, and salvation.

We are told, "The reason the Son of God appeared was to destroy the devil's work" (1 John 3:8). Aware of the painful death that awaited Him, Jesus came willingly to destroy the effects of the Curse and to set in motion the Father's plan to reverse the Curse. God will not abandon His creation, He will restore it to better than "as new" condition.

Jesus performed many miracles. He gave sight to the blind and hearing to the deaf. Jesus strengthened the legs of the feeble and caused the lame to walk again. He removed leprous sores and skin became clean. He cast out demons and revived a sickened mind to be right minded. He stopped the flow of blood from a middle-aged woman and returned the dead to life. These miracles, and many more, confirmed and validated His teaching ministry, but even more significantly, they communicated that God is in the business of restoration.

Christ's miracles are miracles of restoration – restoration to health, restoration to life, to freedom from fear and demons, and to abundance. He has seen what the Curse did to everything He proclaimed to be good, and He refuses to turn His creation over to Satan. God is in the business of making all things new.

Consider the word redemption. It means to buy back what was formerly owned. Reconciliation is the reestablishment of a prior friendship. Resurrection is to become physically alive and whole again after death. These are the works Jesus came to do.

These days the restoration of old stuff is a big deal. Numerous television shows highlight the restoration of cars and homes. Reclaimed wood is in fashion and a current rage in home decor. Old growth redwood is in high demand and steadily increasing in value. What is fascinating is that things restored have significantly increased worth. I marvel at 50 and 60-year-old cars, restored to showroom condition, that auction off for hundreds of thousands of dollars – prices far beyond their original showroom sticker prices.

In high school, I owned a 1967 Chevy El Camino. I paid around $1,000 for it from the original owner. Today, if restored to Concours (pristine) condition it would be worth $30,000. I would delight in having one because it would bring me back to a time lost forever; a time before the pressures of college and work, before mortgage payments and dirty diapers. A time before 911, terrorism, and moral decline. A time when businesses closed on the Sabbath to honor God. When it comes to restored cars, that which was left to rust, and decay, is now redeemed. So, it will be with us and with every square foot of the universe. God will redeem everything. The Curse will be reversed!

I severely broke my right ankle when I was 21 years old. I lived with stiffness and pain most of my adult life. Ultimately, the pain became unbearable, and cortisone shots became routine. That is until ankle replacement surgery became available. While I don't have a new right ankle, I do have a replacement right ankle and can once again live pain-free and active enough to play basketball, ride a bike and hike the wilderness. I have a new lease on life that causes me to crave the complete makeover that awaits my resurrection.

The humanistic concept is that everything is evolving into a higher, perfected state of existence. What we experience, however, is the decline of many things, including morality. Sin is expanding and polluting more of the human experience. What was once good is now deemed to be evil. What was once spoken of as evil is now said to be good. The light of righteousness is mistaken for the darkness of evil, and the darkness of evil is mistaken for light. Without the intervention of Jesus Christ, humankind would be doomed. But praise God for the hope we have in Him!

We are promised, "See, I will create new heavens and a new earth. The former things will not be remembered, nor will they come to mind" (Isaiah 65:17). This blue celestial ball we presently live on is wearing out, and the love we have for one another is growing cold. When the

Curse is finally broken, the former things in our relationships such as suspicion, fear, deceit, arrogance, posturing, belittling, envy, jealousy, pretense and more, will be forgotten because they are the result of the fall of mankind. The Curse is real, but the good news is that it is temporary.

The Beatles song *Getting Better* has a chorus that goes like this, "I've got to admit it's getting better (Better), A little better all the time (It can't get no worse)." It is one of pop culture's biggest lies. One of the most significant promises comes not from this world, but from the Bible: Jesus is returning to make all things new.

I once traveled to India and stayed overnight in New Delhi, a city in a land of enchantment with over 21,000,000 inhabitants. I was expecting crowded conditions, but what I was not expecting was the gross air pollution. It appeared thick enough to cut with a knife, and the locals told me that it never goes away, as though the city is cursed.

On the other hand, I've traveled to Yellowstone, Zion, Bryce Canyon, Moab, and Yosemite National Parks. The beauty is breathtaking. I can only imagine when the New Earth appears the sights, we see will leave us utterly speechless. Once again, a time is coming when we will have access to food and water with minimal labor and without cost. We will work for the sheer pleasure of it. We will have time to pursue every creative aspiration of our heart. Our bucket list will not be impeded. We will please and delight God with the new skills and abilities we develop. People, culture, the Earth and the universe will once again be as God intended.

Without the promise of the Curse being reversed, we are doomed. Isaiah, the prophet, declares, "All of us have become like one who is unclean, and all our righteous acts are like filthy rags; we all shrivel up like a leaf, and like the wind our sins sweep us away" (Isaiah 64:6).

But Christ offers us hope, the hope Paul the Apostle captured when he wrote, "Therefore, if anyone is in Christ, the new creation has come: The old has gone, the new is here!" (2 Corinthians 5:17).

The vivid contrast of earthly eras and of the Curse being reversed is captured in this beautiful poem called *Restored* by James Pusey:

"All hope is lost
And it is no longer true that
I will live in peace and harmony with my God
It is almost beyond imagining but
Perfect days of walking with him in Paradise
Are over and now I am destined for
Days of separation and longing for my true home
My sin is beyond God's grace to forgive
I have come to realize that it is foolish to believe that
God could accept me after all that I had done
How can it be? To think that
All my prayers went unheard
How foolish it was to believe that
He loves me
There is nothing left to do but declare that

I am lost without hope and future
And I can no longer believe that
I will be restored

When sin came
It brought death

But Jesus Christ the Son of God died in our place and
It brought life
He rose again and everything turned upside down.

I will be restored
And I can no longer believe that
I am lost without hope and future
There is nothing left to do but declare that
He loves me
How foolish it was to believe that
All my prayers went unheard
How can it be? To think that
God could accept me after all that I had done
I have come to realize that it is foolish to believe that
My sin is beyond God's grace to forgive
Days of separation and longing for my true home
Are over and now I am destined for
Perfect days of walking with him in Paradise
It is almost beyond imagining but
I will live in peace and harmony with my God
And it is no longer true that
All hope is lost."[21]

The power of Christ's resurrection is enough to not only remake us but also able to reconstruct every inch of the universe. DNA will be perfected, and there will be no more disease, deformities, diabetes, dementia, cancer, high blood pressure or any other human ailment. Mountains, rivers, plants, stars, and galaxies will be made new. All things affected by the fall of mankind will be restored to original condition. Things will no longer get worse or wear out.

CHAPTER 9 - LIFE IN PARADISE

"Life is not measured by the number of breaths we take, but by the moments that take our breath away."

Maya Angelou

Most people do not realize that Paradise and Heaven are two distinct places. If we die anytime soon, we will spend time in both places. Most use the term Heaven and Paradise interchangeably, yet there are distinctions between the two. Since time will be spent in both places, it is intriguing to explore these differences and what life in each location will be like.

Suppose I was traveling in a foreign land with three other people who live in my county, yet all from different towns. In my case, this may be Scotts Valley, Santa Cruz, Boulder Creek, and Watsonville. These towns are contained within Santa Cruz County in California. Imagine we were in an international airport waiting for our gate to open to return home, and a stranger asks us where we are heading. We could say California, which would be correct but not precise.

Furthermore, before we arrived "home" we would be making a layover, say in New York. We could say we were headed to New York, but our stay there would only be a temporary delay. So it is with Paradise and Heaven.

Paradise will be our layover destination. Heaven will be our home, and God will dwell in both locations. The distinction will be the form in which we reside with Him and the timing of when this will take place. This Chapter explores our first stop – Paradise.

Heaven will become our eternal dwelling place only after the following events occur: Jesus returns a second time, He creates a New Heaven and a New Earth, and He summons the resurrection of our bodies from the grave.

These things will happen at "the renewal of all things" (Matthew 19:28). This is a future date known as the "Day of the Lord." Peter teaches us to be prepared, for "the day of the Lord will come like a thief. The heavens will disappear with a roar; the elements will be destroyed by fire, and the earth and everything done in it will be laid bare. Since everything will be destroyed in this way, what kind of people ought you to be? You ought to live holy and godly lives as you look forward to the day of God and speed its coming. That day will bring about the destruction of the heavens by fire, and the elements will melt in the heat. But in keeping with his promise we are looking forward to a new heaven and a new earth, where righteousness dwells" (2 Peter 3:10-13).

The destruction by fire has similarities to the devastation of the global flood. Water is a cleansing agent which God used to wipe clean the face of the Earth in Noah's day. Fire is a refining agent which God will use as a purifying element in the future.

In the meantime, remember that if we think of "Heaven" as the place where God presently dwells, then the statement of going to Heaven immediately after we die is true, it's just not precise.

Paradise as a physical location is mentioned three times in the New Testament. When sin entered the human experience, Adam and Eve were banished from its habitat. But God did not destroy Paradise. It exists today.

We may conjecture where it is, perhaps it has been relocated to a different part of the universe, or it is still on Earth but hidden from our sight. Some theologians, citing Hebrews, Chapter 8:5, (They serve at a sanctuary that is a copy and shadow of what is in heaven.) suggest that the present Earth is only a shadowland of physical reality. We may guess at its location, but we are not presently granted the right to know where it is. What is important to remember is that it is a real, present, physical place.

John recorded a later scene in Revelation that, when observed and studied, reveals a great deal to us about Paradise. I was taught in seminary to approach Scripture much like a Crime Scene Investigator – to look carefully at everything recorded and allow the text to tell its story. In Revelation, Chapter 6, John records an encounter with the martyrs who had been slain for their testimony of Jesus's work in their lives. This scene has much to say about what Paradise is like.

"When he opened the fifth seal, I saw under the altar the souls of those who had been slain because of the word of God and the testimony they had maintained" (Revelation 6:9).

These souls are people who once lived on Earth. Real people who have been sent to Paradise. There is continuity from one life to the next, and these souls are remembered for their life and death on Earth. This shows that in Paradise our identity is maintained, and our life is remembered. The testimony we are writing, our service and sacrifice will be remembered. I wonder what you will be remembered for?

"They called out in a loud voice, 'How long, Sovereign Lord, holy and true until you judge the inhabitants of the earth and avenge our blood?'" (Revelation 6:10).

These souls could verbally express themselves which requires vocal cords, lungs, a mouth and intellect (a brain) to do so. The fact that their voice was raised indicated rationality, emotion, and passion. These attributes point to the possession of some transitional body. Not the body we lived in on Earth, and not our yet-to-be resurrected body, but a temporary body. And did you notice they had a "loud voice" not loud voices? In this life, we have an enormous number of things that divide us, including but not limited to the color of our skin, our nationality, language, wealth, education, sexual orientation, political bent and so forth. In

Paradise, we have a picture of unity. Isn't that what we desperately desire here on Earth?

Evidently, they remember the manner of their death, and they saw martyrdom continuing on Earth. They were fully aware of God, each other, and the situation on Earth. John records them praying, pleading with God, to act on their behalf and on behalf of those who were suffering. They had an audience with God and possessed the relational freedom to ask Him questions. They sought answers to the things they did not know.

In Paradise, we will not be all-knowing, but we will be ever learning. We can safely state that in Paradise we too will have direct access to God, our memories will be clear, and we will be aware of what is presently happening on Earth.

"Then each of them was given a white robe, and they were told to wait a little longer, until the full number of their fellow servants, their brothers and sisters, were killed just as they had been" (Revelation 6:11). White robes further reinforce the idea of transitional bodies – disembodied spirits don't wear clothes.

Not only could they ask questions of God, but God answered them. In this two-way dialogue, the martyrs gain new information and are told to wait, indicating that they experience time (and they learn over time). They are seen presently existing with the ability to look at the atrocities of what is happening on Earth. The Voice of the Martyrs – a Christian non-profit organization that tracts persecution in the Church –

reports that more than 90,000 people die each year for their testimony of Christ. God knows the name and story of each one of them.

In Revelation Chapter 6, Jesus asks for patience before He returns, as we see that more martyrs will have to die before God acts to bring the present era to an end. We may be one of those who will be martyred. You may be the final martyr – it is possible.

We also observe that those living on Earth, and those in Paradise, are part of one Church – the living and the dead are brothers and sisters indicating that there is no wall of separation in God's family. Therefore, we have seen that in Paradise we will experience time, we will gain new knowledge, and we will exist with those on Earth as single members of the Bride of Christ.

Though this scene is a snapshot of those martyred, I believe the physical properties described pertain to those not martyred as well. People such as the repentant thief, the beggar Lazarus, those taken captive by Jesus from the depths of Hades, and all who have died in Christ since His resurrection. Our loved ones who accepted Jesus and have died are included as well.

The observations we've seen are supported and enhanced by additional insights found elsewhere in the Bible. The Bible does not give us any idea on whether the deceased in Hades can or cannot see on Earth. Since the martyrs in Paradise see what is happening on Earth, the argument can be made that our deceased loved ones in Paradise may presently look at our lives. They likely are witnesses to what we experience, both good and bad, holy and unholy.

The writer of Hebrews calls our attention to a "great cloud of witnesses," which may very well be those presently located in Paradise. The illustration is given of spectators cheering us on as we approach and then cross the finish line of life. Our loved friends and family members may be watching us and cheering us on. Consider the scene, "Therefore, since we are surrounded by such a great cloud of witnesses, let us throw off everything that hinders and the sin that so easily entangles" (Hebrews 12:1).

When any of us here on Earth repent and receive Jesus's work of salvation on our behalf, this cloud of witnesses rejoices. Notice in Luke, Chapter 15, it is not the angels who rejoice. Instead, it is others who rejoice *in the presence of* the angels. "In the same way, I tell you, there is rejoicing in the presence of the angels of God over one sinner who repents" (Luke 15:10). Could it be the souls of those who have died and are now in Paradise who do the rejoicing? It appears so.

It is natural to ponder then if the deceased can see what is happening on Earth. How do they process the evil, pain, and suffering they may see? Would not the awareness of such cause them to be sad, just as our hearts break for the wicked and tragic things, we are made aware of here?

It's challenging to maintain joy when we hear of murder, rape, theft, cancer, accidents and such. Perhaps if there were no awareness of the activities taking place on Earth, there would be undiluted joy and happiness in Paradise. It is hard to comprehend how there could be "no more tears, mourning, crying or pain" (Revelation 21:4). With the awareness that is present. What about the old saying, "Ignorance is bliss?"

Happiness in Paradise is not based on ignorance, but rather on perspective. Surely God sees all that is taking place and His joy is not diminished. The same can be said of the angels who are front row witnesses to the judgment of the wicked that will take place (Revelation 4:9-10). And yet they do not have any less happiness. Abraham and Lazarus saw the rich man's agonies in Hades, and there is no indication that their joy was diluted.

In our present state of ignorance, we lack the wisdom to see things as God sees them. The perspective we will be given once we die will be fundamental in mysteriously changing our tears into joy.

Many faith traditions pray for the dead, which is not found in the original autographic Biblical text; in Hebrew and Greek.[22] The Bible is clear that the fate of the dead is sealed, and further petitioning on their behalf will not move the throne of God to respond.

However, it is legitimate to consider that the dead pray for us who remain here on Earth. This could explain why there is so much rejoicing over a single sinner who repents. Perhaps this is the result of a father, sister, grandmother or best friend whose petition has led to the events surrounding a decision of faith. We've already seen how those martyred are praying as they call for an end to martyrdom. In any case, we know for sure that there is at least one person who prays for us, the Lord Jesus. "Who then is the one who condemns? No one. Christ Jesus who died—more than that, who was raised to life—is at the right hand of God and is also interceding for us" (Romans 8:34).

The possession of memory after death is an intriguing thought. Without memory how could anyone be required to give an account, not only of our sins but also of every word we've ever spoken? "But I tell you that everyone will have to give account on the day of judgment for every empty word they have spoken" (Matthew 12:36). Our memories will be so vividly sharp that not a soul will be able to say, "I have no recollection of ever saying that."

Please understand some memories stay with us forever. Other memories must be recalled by others. They remain buried within and must be remembered. I can tell you that there are many things I would like to forget: shameful things and embarrassing situations permanently. Although I will be held accountable for what I have done, my comfort is in knowing that God will not remember my sins as they have been covered by Christ's action of the cross. "Their sins and lawless acts I will remember no more" (Hebrews 10:17).

The possibility that we will be able to remember our sins, along with all aspects of our earthly lives, will bring greater love and devotion to God. We will be able to see how He worked in our lives and how great His salvation indeed is. We will see without any uncertainty that we do not belong in Paradise by our merits, but by His alone.

If we truly believe God's testimony that we have been given eternal life, then I ask us what realm are we living in? Do we keep our focus on earthly things or on heavenly things? The more we can live with Paradise in mind, the more prepared and excited we will be to arrive there.

CHAPTER 10 - REWARDS

"Paul, we are going to kill you. That is cool, then I
will go to Christ. Ok Paul, we are going to let you live.
That is great, then I can witness Christ. Ok, then we
will torture you. That is fine, then I will receive a
reward in Heaven one day."

Tony Evans

Once humankind is restored to the New Earth, we
will regain our original place as co-rulers with Christ of
the universe. Of course, Christ could rule all by himself,
but He shares that responsibility with all the redeemed.
The degree of trust we will have in the next life will be a
matter of our faithfulness in this life. The Bible indicates
that our responsibility in Heaven will be presented as a
reward.

We will find our ultimate, eternal purpose to be
reigning with Christ over His restored creation. The
redeemed of the Lord will one day serve God under a
Kingdom united. When Jesus renews all things, He also
renews mankind's original elevated role.

"... with your blood you purchased for God persons
from every tribe and language and people and nation.

You have made them to be a kingdom and priests to serve our God, and they will reign on the earth" (Revelation 5:9-10).

The reign of God and the reign of man will continue to radiate outward from the New Heaven / New Earth as the entire universe is governed and submitted to Him. In Heaven, we will experience the great promise given to us through the Prophet Isaiah, who indicated that God's government will continue to grow. This will happen either through the creation of new territories, or the submission of regions previously ungoverned.

"For to us a child is born, to us a son is given, and the government will be on his shoulders. And he will be called Wonderful Counselor, Mighty God, Everlasting Father, Prince of Peace. Of the greatness of his government and peace there will be no end" (Isaiah 9:6-7).

Jesus communicates that there will be various levels of responsibility in Heaven, as determined by how a person lived their life for God here on the present Earth. Jesus indicated this in His parable of talents recorded in Luke, Chapter 19. He showed that future responsibility of taking charge over cities was measured out on differing scales according to a servant's present trustworthiness.

"While they were listening to this, he went on to tell them a parable, because he was near Jerusalem and the people thought that the kingdom of God was going to appear at once. He said: "A man of noble birth went to a distant country to have himself appointed king and then to return. So he called ten of his servants and gave them ten minas. 'Put this money to work,' he said, 'until I come back.' But his subjects hated him and sent a delegation after him to say, 'We don't want this man to be our king.' "He was made king, however, and returned home. Then he sent for the servants to whom he had given the money, in order to find out what they had gained with it. "The first one came and said, 'Sir, your mina has earned ten more.' 'Well done, my good servant!' his master replied. 'Because you have been trustworthy in a very small matter, take charge of ten cities.' The second came and said, 'Sir, your mina has earned five more.' "His master answered, 'You take charge of five cities'" (Luke 19:11-24).

Because we will be sinless in Heaven when rewards are handed out, there will be no thoughts of pride, envy or superiority; no one will feel worthless or insignificant, and no one will feel arrogant. Won't that be refreshing? Regarding heavenly rewards, we should long for them. While rewards should not be our highest Biblical motive, they are none the less motives worth investigating.

My Apple iPhone has a screen time feature that tracks and reports the time I spend on my phone. It shows the time making and receiving phone calls, using mail, searching the internet, playing games, social networking, reading, and more. It is a feature to which the marketers devote a high level of interest, and which they are likely tracking. I try my best to limit my time to productive activities only, but time is still wasted. The current report over the past week was an average of 56 minutes on my phone every day. Not only does Apple know how I spent those 56 minutes, but this information is stored in Heaven as well, just like the other 23 hours and 04 minutes of every day are recorded. Every single minute is important, and those minutes can be used for my benefit or the benefit of others. One of my wife's favorite poems is called, "I have only just a minute" by Dr. Benjamin E. Mays:

> *"I have only just a minute,*
> *Only sixty seconds in it.*
> *Forced upon me, can't refuse it.*
> *Didn't seek it, didn't choose it.*
> *But it's up to me to use it.*
> *I must suffer if I lose it.*
> *Give account if I abuse it.*
> *Just a tiny little minute,*
> *but eternity is in it."*

This poem speaks to the extreme value of time and the responsibility we have to use it wisely. God will hold us accountable for the things we have done; how we used our limited time. Here is what awaits, "For we must all appear before the judgment seat of Christ, so that each of us may receive what is due us for the things done while in the body, whether good or bad" (2 Corinthians 5:10).

Notice these are things which are either good or bad, not good or evil. The word chosen for bad represents the concept of "foolish" or "worthless." Some things done "in the body" can be things that serve God and advance His Kingdom. Other things, indifferent to God and His

Kingdom, are ultimately worthless. The wise person will strive to deposit as much time as possible to those activities that further God's agenda on this planet. We do that by building on the foundation of Jesus Christ as recorded by the Apostle Paul:

For no one can lay any foundation other than the one already laid, which is Jesus Christ. If anyone builds on this foundation using gold, silver, costly stones, wood, hay or straw, their work will be shown for what it is, because the Day will bring it to light. It will be revealed with fire, and the fire will test the quality of each person's work. If what has been built survives, the builder will receive a reward. If it is burned up, the builder will suffer loss but yet will be saved—even though only as one escaping through the flames (see 1 Corinthians 3:11-15).

An honest evaluation of how we spend our time is a profitable exercise. When I lose sight of why I am here and what matters most I tend to chase more stuff and waste more time. I go after that which is bigger, better and in greater quantity. I dream about bucket lists and scheme on accomplishing them before it's too late to do so. How quickly I forget that in Heaven I will have time without limit to pursue every fancy of my imagination.

No prize on earth will match the words of Jesus to His faithful stewards, "His master replied, 'Well done, good and faithful servant! You have been faithful with a few things; I will put you in charge of many things. Come and share your master's happiness!'" (Matthew 25:21). We often refer to the first part of this verse as we long to hear that we've done an excellent job here on Earth. However, the second part is often overlooked which relates the reward of future responsibility in Heaven with present faithfulness on Earth.

I think it is prudent to seek after the rewards God's promises since they are mentioned 22 times in the New Testament. Consider the word reward mentioned in these verses of scripture:

"If you love those who love you, what *reward* will you get? Are not even the tax collectors doing that?" (Matthew 5:46).

"For the Son of Man is going to come in his Father's glory with his angels, and then he will *reward* each person according to what they have done" (Matthew 16:27).

"The one who plants and the one who waters have one purpose, and they will each be *rewarded* according to their own labor. For we are co-workers in God's service; you are God's field, God's building" (1 Corinthians 3:8-9).

The idea of crowns as rewards repeatedly appears in the Bible. Five different crowns are given according to how we respond to different circumstances we may face in this life.

There is the crown that will last forever (see 1 Corinthians 9:25-27), the crown of righteousness (see 2 Timothy 4:8), the crown of life (see James 1:12), the crown of rejoicing (see 1 Thessalonians 2:19), and the crown of glory (see 1 Peter 5:4). Various crowns are given to those who have used the spiritual gifts and abilities God has given them to serve God and His Kingdom faithfully. Crowns are for those who have longed for Christ's appearance and for those who have endured the testing of their faith, even to the point of death. Crowns are also given to those who have participated directly in the saving of souls. Finally, crowns go to those who have faithfully served God's people.

Crowns are worn by kings and queens. They represent authority and responsibility for a specific realm. The rewards of crowns communicate that when the Curse is finally lifted, we will regain the right to rule over God's creation that was initially granted to Adam and Eve.

Some of us are more inclined to follow rather than lead, and we may be apprehensive about being given the responsibility of ruling. However, whatever God puts us in charge of will be fitted perfectly to our skills, passion, ability, and heart. Are you an animal lover? You may very well have duties with animals. Are you a plant lover? A lover of rivers, insects, birds, design, construction, or exploration? Whatever our bent, that will be the direction God sends us. It will be good.

Today, be assured that nothing you do for God is ever lost or wasted. God knows all, and God sees all. He continually searches, looking for those whose hearts are fully committed to Him (see 2 Chronicles 16:9). God is looking for those who are obedient and faithful in what God is calling them to do in this life.

This present life may seem insignificant, but in light of eternity and because of God's evaluation, it is essential and necessary. Whatever we do, we all should work as unto the Lord (see Colossians 3:23). So, let us remain steadfast and unwavering in our commitment to God. We will be rewarded.

A favorite verse that prompts my perseverance, one I've committed to memory and relied on time and time again, is found in Paul's first letter to the church in Corinth. May it likewise encourage you.

"Therefore, my dear brothers and sisters, stand firm. Let nothing move you. Always give yourselves fully to the work of the Lord, because you know that your labor in the Lord is not in vain" (1 Corinthians 15:58).

Paul is asking us to stand firm to prepare us for the outcome of giving all in service to Christ. In this life, those that serve Christ wholeheartedly will encounter opposition, resistance, and discouragement; they will be beaten down. Life can be so incredibly difficult that the temptation will be to give up. Whatever our lot right now, understand God is watching and making a note of those He will reward.

It is imperative that we understand rewards are not related to salvation. Salvation is a gift of God and not dependent on our good works. Paul makes this crystal clear, "For it is by grace you have been saved, through faith—and this is not from yourselves, it is the gift of God— not by works, so that no one can boast" (Ephesians 2:8-9). The reward of faith is salvation, and salvation is gifted not earned. On the other hand, what we do with our salvation is rewarded.

Not only is salvation gifted to us, but the assurance of our salvation is gifted as well. I am confident that when I die, I will go to Paradise. This is not because I devoted my life to pastoring, or have traveled on many mission trips, donated sacrificial amounts of money or attempted to be a good person. Like everyone else, I fall short. I will go to Paradise because I have accepted what Jesus has done for me on the cross. Period. We have God's testimony of this truth.

"And this is the testimony: God has given us eternal life, and this life is in his Son. Whoever has the Son has life; whoever does not have the Son of God does not have life. I write these things to you who believe in the name of the Son of God so that you may know that you have eternal life" (1 John 5:11-13).

Jesus lives in my heart because I have accepted His invitation to enter my heart. Jesus, the Bible relates, longs for us to respond and invite Him in, "Here I am! I stand at the door and knock. If anyone hears my voice and opens the door, I will come in and eat with that person, and they with me" (Revelation 3:20). If we could earn our way into Heaven by our good works, Heaven would ultimately be just like Earth. We would be full of pride and boasting, and we would take credit for our salvation. We would be surprised to see others there, for in our judgment we did not see them as good enough. In time Heaven would be as ugly and sinful as the life we now know.

To repeat, rewards are layered on top of our salvation. Rewards, of both treasure and increased responsibility, are offered by God to a believer based on faithful service rendered _after_ salvation. Our motivation for good works and faithful service is gratitude and adoration. I want to live my life for Jesus in response to what He has done for me. I know I don't deserve Paradise and I can't possibly gain it on my own. However, God who has accepted me and forgiven me now deserves my loyalty and dedication.

CHAPTER 11 - THE BEST IS YET TO COME

"When we are on the beach we only see a small part of the ocean. However, we know that there is much more beyond the horizon. We only see a small part of God's great love, a few jewels of His great riches, but we know that there is much more beyond the horizon. The best is yet to come when we see Jesus face-to-face."

Corrie Ten Boom

Perhaps you share the sentiments of Isaac Asimov who wrote, "I don't believe in an afterlife, so I don't have to spend my whole life fearing hell or fearing heaven even more. For whatever the tortures of hell, I think the boredom of heaven would even be worse."[23] If you're inclined to agree with Mr. Asimov, then this book may be one of the most important books you have ever read. I hope and pray that someday you will change your mind about what the Bible communicates to us about Heaven, not for my benefit but for yours.

To those who are convinced of the biblical view of the afterlife, I say hang on, for the best is yet to come. No matter how good life may be, or how good a life we have spent on this Earth, life will get better in Heaven. Even when life is at its very best, we can expect something far more significant than we can imagine. When comparing this life to an eternity in Heaven, we can proclaim that Earth has nothing we desire, besides God.

Home is the place I am most myself. I am comfortable there. Home is where I spend time with loved ones, connect with my wife and children, host a Bible Study, eat, read and pray, watch my favorite sports team, and schedule the routine parts of my life to live a responsible life. When I am away from home for an extended period, my heart longs to return and to be with the familiar. Humanity appears to be searching for the security of home but is looking for it in all the wrong places. Many of our vices stem from our homesickness for a very particular place.

We are homesick for Heaven and we are yearning for God. We attempt to treat this sickness with whatever we think would alleviate the pain: sex, pornography, alcohol, drugs, reckless spending, craving new, bigger and better things – from homes to cars to clothes to vacations. What we really crave, what we really desire is Jesus and Heaven. As the Psalmist wrote, "Whom have I in heaven but you? And earth has nothing I desire besides you" (Psalm 73:25). Nothing less than Jesus can completely satisfy the human soul. Fortunately, Heaven is our home – let's not forget that!

At the same time, there are things that I enjoy greatly. I am sure the same is true for you. Every Sunday afternoon I play a couple of hours of basketball in my driveway with family and friends. In the winter I love to sit on my living room couch with the wood stove burning, watching my beloved Golden State Warriors wreak havoc on the court. I enjoy sitting down with a good book, especially when on vacation at our favorite mountain lake. And did I mention my delight in a freshly grilled ribeye steak or salmon filet?

How does God feel when I find delight in such things? I think that is a matter of what place they hold in my heart. Surely, they must not replace the joy of knowing Jesus. I see Jesus as the giver of good gifts and the one who grants these things to me (see James 1:17). God is not a killjoy. When I take pleasure in what He provides, it must make Him feel blessed and delighted also. God wants to be acknowledged as the source of joy, much as a parent who buys their child a special Christmas or birthday gift. If the child took delight in it, most parents would not sit around and pout about it. They would be very pleased. Pleased even more when the child expresses gratitude in a meaningful, heartfelt manner.

Like Isaac Asimov, some think that Heaven will be boring because they understand a narrow definition of worshipping God they see as dull. In Heaven, we will worship God continually. Yet, Heaven is not one neverending Church service. The worship in Heaven is higher, broader and more profound than we can ever imagine now.

God will always be first in our thinking. That is the definition of worship that I like to use. And it won't be boring, for lovers do not bore each other. Meeting with

God will be far more exhilarating than anything we have ever experienced.

When I look back on life, I can still sense the awe and wonder of many firsts – my first kiss; the first time I drove a vehicle by myself; the time I co-piloted a single engine airplane over the spectacular San Francisco Bay; my ride in a 600+ horsepower Ferrari on a professional racetrack at breakneck speeds. My heart still beats fast when I recall these events. Yet, God is more fascinating than any human experience or encounter. When I see Him face to face, I hope I remember to breathe.

Eternal life will be far greater than enjoying forever our most beautiful times on Earth. Those moments that stick out as the pinnacle of our experiences. Not only those with high adrenaline but also the peaceful moments, the ones with the sun shining; a warm, gentle breeze, soothing sights and sounds, pleasant company with our health strong and the pressures silenced. Such moments are rare, but they do occur, and when they do, they are pleasant appetizers of more to come. It's what we long for – a world with all the beauty and none of the ugliness; all life's positives and none of the negatives.

Since Heaven will be the restored, renewed, and recreated Earth, we can learn much by examining the original creation and projecting that understanding into the future. At creation, every day God declared that what He had created was good. Over and over we read, "God said let there be ... and it was good."[24] At the conclusion of all His creative work, He declared it to be "very good" (Genesis 1:31).

A dramatic shift in God's evaluation arises when He sees that man is all alone, and thus He makes that proclamation that to be alone was "not good" (Genesis 2:18). We are created in the image and likeness of God as relational beings, and we need other people to relate to. That is why God graciously created the woman – she was to be a companion to the man and together they were to complement and complete each other. We were made in the image of God and God thrives in His triune relationships. The Father has a relationship with the Son, who has a relationship with the Holy Spirit, who has a relationship with the Father.

Our relationships are a gift and one of our most valuable possessions. Family and friends help make this life worth living. In the context of our relationships, we are loved, accepted, understood, comforted and challenged. Sure, relationships can also be our most significant source of difficulty and frustration. One day the relational dysfunction caused by the Curse will be reversed.

Of all connections, marriage is the most sacred. Not that all people need to feel complete only if married. I believe singleness is also a gift from God for those who are equipped for it (see 1 Corinthians 7:25-40). The uniqueness of marriage is that it represents the relationship Christ has with the Church (see Ephesians 5:25-33). Marriage was instituted by God to reflect the image of God's great love, provision, care and leadership of His bride, the Church.

Contrary to what some believe, the Bible does teach that there will be marriage in Heaven. However, there will be only one marriage – that is the union between Christ and His bride, the Church (see Ephesians 5:31-32). While we will be a part of one large family, individuals will not be married to each other. For those who are currently happily married and cannot imagine life without their marital partner, this may throw a dark cloud on the whole concept of Heaven. We may be married to our very best friend, and naturally, we want that special relationship to continue. Just because we won't be married in Heaven, does not mean that we can't be, or won't still be, best of friends.

On the other hand, for those in a challenging marriage, one filled with strife, bickering and constant tension, the release from your union may sound like welcomed news. You may find yourself hanging onto your relationship out of duty or obligation. It's unfortunate but true that some marriages are like this. Heaven will change everything.

According to God's design, sex and marriage go together. Logically, if there is no marriage in Heaven, there will be no sex in Heaven. Again, depending on your age and life experiences, this may be highly disappointing, or highly anticipated. As much as continuity from this life to the next is revealed in the Scriptures, this seems to be an exception to that rule. There is continuity of breath, of our personalities, of our bodies, of our memories and more. For most who are married, it is difficult to consider life any other way. But there will be no continuity of marriage as we know it.

In marriage, and in marital sex, we find intimacy and pleasure. These are things declared "good" by God. Based on the nature and character of God, we must put our trust in Him that He will provide intimacy, pleasure, and closeness in some greater, more meaningful and enjoyable expression. Intimacy is the highest statement of sex, and I love how my friend Ron describes intimacy. He rephrases it as "into-me-see." We will be open and transparent. There will be nothing to hide and no shame to conceal. We will be seen for who we are, and more importantly, loved and cherished for who we are.

It is impossible to know what the replacement for intimate sexual expression may be, but we do know that God withholds no good thing from those who are sinless (see Psalm 84:11). Marriage partners in this life will still be best friends in the next life. Sex will be replaced with something better. Remember, the "sex" we know is not a basic human need like water, food or oxygen. Naturally, sex is necessary for procreation, but the Scriptures are silent on reproduction in Heaven. There will be no sex, and yet relational intimacy will be focal and greatly amplified.

There are people, even married people, who are not as concerned about marriage in the afterlife as they are about seeing their loved pets again. A common question is, "Will my pets be in Heaven?" I long to see again the pets I once owned – Nakita, my chocolate lab; Rainbow Cheerio, our family's first cat; Oliver, the most adorable tabby ever; plus, the other dogs, cats, rabbits and chickens we've owned. The Bible does not provide a direct answer to this question, but there is an abundance of evidence to suggest this will be the case.

Animals are Earth's second most important inhabitants. Like man, they were formed out of the ground. No other element of creation was made from the ground. As He did for man, God placed in animals the breath of life - a trait which only animals and humans share (Genesis 2:19). Before the Curse, animals were given as companions and helpers to mankind – they were not presented as sources of food and clothing.

Animals have been included at crucial moments in the history of the world. At creation, they were present with Adam and Eve. In the global flood, they were preserved with Noah. Animals surrounded Jesus at his birth. Animals are considered flesh and the promise is given that "All flesh will see the salvation of God" (Luke 3:6 NASU).

During the global flood, God saved humanity and the animals. After the waters receded, God made a covenant, known as the Noahic Covenant, that He would never again send a flood to destroy the earth. What stuns me is that God also made this covenant with the animals.

"I now establish my covenant with you and with your descendants after you and with every living creature that was with you—the birds, the livestock and all the wild animals, all those that came out of the ark with you— every living creature on earth. I establish my covenant with you: Never again will all life be destroyed by the waters of a flood; never again will there be a flood to destroy the earth" (Genesis 9:9-11).

I have seen my own children become overjoyed when a new pet came to live with us. I delighted in their joy much like God delights in our happiness. It is a reasonable bridge to cross in saying there will be animals in Heaven, and possibly even our beloved pets. If it would please us, and please God, for us to have a restored pet in Heaven, that well might be reason enough for God to permit it. The Psalmist declared, "In your presence there is fullness of joy" (Psalm 16:11 NKJV).

However, I want to be clear on the point that Jesus did not come to die for animals. Animals cannot sin, and the death they experience is the result of mankind's sin. As humanity suffers so do the animals and the rest of creation. There is nothing in the entire universe that has not been stained by the Curse. Just as creation will be made new, so too animals will be restored. The prophet Isaiah declared:

"The wolf will live with the lamb, the leopard will lie down with the goat, the calf and the lion and the yearling together; and a little child will lead them. The cow will feed with the bear, their young will lie down together, and the lion will eat straw like the ox. The infant will play near the cobra's den, the young child will put its hand into the viper's nest. They will neither harm nor destroy on all my holy mountain, for the earth will be filled with the knowledge of the Lord as the waters cover the sea" (Isaiah 11:6-9).

In Heaven, we will laugh and sing, make music, and create; we will have complete joy. Based on how refreshing it is to sleep, I will go out on a limb and even say we will know what deep sleep is as well. We will work for the pure joy of it, we will run, walk, rest, play sports, and, best of all, relate perfectly to each other and to God. We will continually learn and develop new skills.

We have hope in Jesus; a hope which does not disappoint. We must acknowledge our life here presently is short. We should never lose sight of the fact that the best is yet to come. Are we living more for today or for tomorrow? Each of us needs to make the most significant impact possible for the Kingdom of God every day. What awaits is the life we have always wanted.

CHAPTER 12 - HEAVEN WILL BLOW YOUR MIND

"Everybody wants to go to heaven. We are all curious to know where it is, what it looks like, who's there, and what they wear and do."

Joni Eareckson Tada

Most have little idea of what Heaven, our permanent home, will really be like. We have just enough information revealed to us in the Bible, however, to know that it will be spectacular far beyond our limited comprehension. In short, it will blow your mind. Synonyms for that phrase include impress, overwhelm, move, stir, affect, touch, sweep someone off their feet, awe, leave speechless, take someone's breath away, spellbind, hypnotize, fascinate, stagger, floor, amaze, and astonish. Heaven will do just that.

What we really want is a place to call home with Jesus at the center of it all. A home with all the splendor of what we presently know yet without any of the corruption. We picture Heaven with Jesus as a dwelling place void of the Curse, without sin, lacking the strife of personal, relational problems and the disappointment of unmet expectations. Welcome to our New Earth, also known as the New Heaven.

God destroyed the world one time already in the global flood, and He will do it again with a refining fire. Sin will be purged, and newness of life will return. Just as the flood did not make the Earth uninhabitable, so the fire will not end in desolation. Out of the ashes will rise beauty, glory, magnificence, and wonder.

One of the final promises God has made to us is about the creation of a New Heaven and a New Earth, the center of which will be the New Jerusalem – the greatest city ever. The New Jerusalem will come down from above to rest on the New Earth which suggests that the New Heaven and the New Earth will converge into one new location.

"Then I saw 'a new heaven and a new earth,' for the first heaven and the first earth had passed away, and there was no longer any sea. I saw the Holy City, the new Jerusalem, coming down out of heaven from God, prepared as a bride beautifully dressed for her husband. And I heard a loud voice from the throne saying, 'Look! God's dwelling place is now among the people, and he will dwell with them. They will be his people, and God himself will be with them and be their God. 'He will wipe every tear from their eyes. There will be no more death' or mourning or crying or pain, for the old order of things has passed away.' He who was seated on the throne said, 'I am making everything new!' Then he said, 'Write this down, for these words are trustworthy and true'" (Revelation 21:1-5).

God will make everything new. He will not abandon His original design. Instead, He will restore Earth to its original condition. The eternal Heaven will be familiar for it will be located on Earth. The restored Earth will have familiar geography, if not familiar locations. I'm speculating, since I live in California, I will once again see Monterey Bay, the San Francisco Bay Area, Lake Tahoe, redwood trees, coastal oak trees, sunrises, and sunsets, in vivid, undiminished color and clarity. The names may change, but the locations will remain. And if the locations are gone, then similar, recognizable geography will replace them.

I am aware that the Apostle John tells us there will no longer be any sea. But I interpret this to mean no more sea as the ancient world knew the sea. The sea was dreadful. From it, enemies seemingly out of nowhere, would arrive to destroy and plunder. Voyagers would depart in large ships never to be seen again. Seasoned sailors would spin tales of terrifying tempests and monstrous creatures. It would be quite unappealing to include these elements descriptive of the New Earth. But a calm sea, crystal blue, teaming with playful life is a thing of peace and beauty.

I remember the first time my wife and I vacationed in Hawaii, and we stayed the entire time on the island of Maui. We rented a car and drove to a remote beach well off the beaten path. As we desired to capture the primal beauty of the island, we parked our vehicle and then walked several hundred yards through lush vegetation. In awe, we came to an opening which offered a panoramic view of the white sand beach and small cove below.

My immediate thoughts drew me to Heaven. I received a foretaste of what it will be like. However, as picturesque as it was, I was looking at a beach that had suffered through the fall of mankind and all that the Curse represented. As beautiful and poster-like as it was, I could begin to imagine this beach in its original pristine condition. God treated us to a prelude of Heaven.

Sit on the thought that everything will be made new. Impurities, gone. Imperfections, eliminated. Rust and decay, destroyed. Things will no longer wear out. Death will no longer lie in wait for its next victim. DNA will be flawless. Disease and sickness will be forever sidelined.

I love the promise that God's dwelling place will be among His people – just as it was before the Curse. The first two Chapters of the Bible and the last two Chapters mirror each other. The Bible ends how it starts; it starts with creation and ends with the new creation. Our story will continue.

The capital city of our future dwelling spot will be the New Jerusalem. Its immensity is matched only by its magnificence.

"And he carried me away in the Spirit to a mountain great and high, and showed me the Holy City, Jerusalem, coming down out of heaven from God. It shone with the glory of God, and its brilliance was like that of a very precious jewel, like a jasper, clear as crystal. It had a great, high wall with twelve gates, and with twelve angels at the gates. On the gates were written the names of the twelve tribes of Israel. There were three gates on the east, three on the north, three on the south and three on the west. The wall of the city had twelve foundations, and on them were the names of the twelve apostles of the Lamb.

The angel who talked with me had a measuring rod of gold to measure the city, its gates, and its walls. The city was laid out like a square, as long as it was wide. He measured the city with the rod and found it to be 12,000 stadia in length, and as wide and high as it is long. The angel measured the wall using human measurement, and it was 144 cubits thick. The wall was made of jasper, and the city of pure gold, as pure as glass. The foundations of the city walls were decorated with every kind of precious stone. The first foundation was jasper, the second sapphire, the third agate, the fourth emerald, the fifth onyx, the sixth ruby, the seventh chrysolite, the eighth beryl, the ninth topaz, the tenth turquoise, the eleventh jacinth, and the twelfth amethyst. The twelve gates were twelve pearls, each gate made of a single pearl. The great street of the city was of gold, as pure as transparent glass.

I did not see a temple in the city, because the Lord God Almighty and the Lamb are its temple. The city does not need the sun or the moon to shine on it, for the glory of God gives it light, and the Lamb is its lamp. The nations will walk by its light, and the kings of the earth will bring their splendor into it. On no day will its gates ever be shut, for there will be no night there. The glory and honor of the nations will be brought into it. Nothing impure will ever enter it, nor will anyone who does what is shameful or deceitful, but only those whose names are written in the Lamb's book of life" (Revelation 21:10-27).

This world knows some great cities – places such as London, New York, Tokyo, Dubai and the like. But the New Jerusalem will have greatness so far beyond what we know that every one of us will be blown away by it.

Interestingly, fifteen times in the last two Chapters of Revelation the place where God and His people will dwell together is called a city. Cities are familiar to us. Every city has its distinct design, architecture, and culture and the New Jerusalem is no exception. It is described as having walls, gates, streets, and a river. This city is not some unseen spiritual realm but rather a real physical location. In the New Jerusalem, there will be no temple because all will have access to God's presence. The greatest miracle of all will be our access to God.

Today, we do not measure distances, as the angel did, in stadia or cubits, so we must convert to a more familiar unit of measure. In miles, the New Jerusalem is approximately 1,380 miles in length, width, and height. A superstructure of all super-structures. A city of this size at ground level would be over 1,900,000 square miles. That is an area 50% greater than India! We don't know how many people will end up in Heaven, but we do know that Jesus did tell us to enter the small gate leading to the narrow path for wide is the path that leads to destruction (see Matthew 7:13-14).

We do have expert estimates of how many people have been born and one time lived on this Earth, and that number is just over 108 billion people.[25] Arbitrarily, we could guess that 10% of the population who have ever lived will end up in Heaven. The 10% / 90% ratio seems to fit the narrow and wide ratio Jesus was talking about. But perhaps the number is higher or lower. For the sake of argument, let's stick with 10% or about 10.8 billion people in Heaven. Would the New Jerusalem be large enough to contain them?

The New Jerusalem may be in the shape of a cube, or it may be in the form of a pyramid. The description provided allows for both interpretations. I favor considering it as the shape of a cube primarily because the Holy of Holies in the Tabernacle (the place God would meet with the High Priest in the Old Testament period) was a perfect 30-foot cube.

Since the New Jerusalem is exceptionally high (not only long and wide), it most certainly has different levels. If each story had a ceiling height of 50 feet, then this city would have over 145,000 floors; enough space that each of the 10.8 billion occupants would be allocated 25.7 square miles. If the city were a pyramid shape and not a cube, each occupant would still have an allocation of 8.5 square miles. Since God's desire from the beginning has been that none should perish, (see 2 Peter 3:9). 108 billion people could fit in such a pyramid and still have just under 1 square mile per person, or 544 acres each! The enormity of the New Jerusalem is mind-boggling.

Even if the dimensions given to us in Revelation are figurative and not literal, the Biblical author is conveying that the home of God's people will be substantial and roomy. Since it is constructed of pure gold, it would be opulent as well.

When Jesus departed this world, He said that he was going to prepare a place for each one of us, as His Father's house (the New Jerusalem) has many rooms (see John 14:2). If the creation account was accomplished in 7 days, it is incomprehensible what Jesus could create in 2,000 years. It will blow your mind.

But the New Jerusalem, while being the capital city, will only be one of the presumably many cities. In speaking of rewards, Jesus told his faithful servants that they would have charge of many cities. "'Well done, my good servant!' his master replied. 'Because you have been trustworthy in a very small matter, take charge of ten cities.' "The second came and said, 'Sir, your mina has earned five more.' "His master answered, 'You take charge of five cities'" (Luke 19:17-19).

Indeed, there must be other cities for we are told that the "kings of the earth" will bring their splendor into it. These kings must have their own cities to rule. Heaven in my mind keeps on getting bigger.

We are also told that the twelve gates to the city will remain open and citizens of the New Earth will always be welcomed, free to come and go as they wish. These gates will be approximately 300 miles apart. In ancient days, the city gates were places where people gathered to conduct business: tell stories, similar to our modern coffee shops. Coming and going, we will find ourselves stopping at these gates to tell our stories. We will have a universe to explore and countless stories to share upon our return with unlimited time to tell them. Stories that we will be eager to share and eager to hear.

I am not a city person. I attended all four of my college years in San Francisco, and that was about as much city as I could take. You may be just the opposite which is just fine; we will all be accommodated in the New Jerusalem. I like to travel and explore and will take the open country over high density living every time. Perhaps I'm biased by the crime, pollution, sirens, traffic fatalities, garbage and sections of poverty in most cities. The only cities I have ever experienced are ones under the Curse. But the New Jerusalem will be filled with natural wonders, magnificent architecture, and exciting culture. I just may become a city dweller.

Notice the foundations of New Jerusalem: multiple foundations made of precious jewels. A structure's greatest strength is its foundation. When my children were very small, I built a two-story play structure for them in our backyard. I designed this without proper consideration given to its foundation, and as the structure neared completion, it was flimsy and unstable. Before finishing it, the thought occurred to me that if my children were in this structure during an earthquake, the entire playhouse could come tumbling down, and severe injury or death would result. So, I tore the playhouse down and started over, beginning with the foundation.

The final structure was super sturdy and well worth the effort to build it right.

As fate would have it, my children and several other children in the neighborhood, were inside that playhouse when the most massive earthquake since 1906 struck the area. The Loma Prieta Earthquake, which hit during game one of the Major League Baseball World Series on October 17, 1989. The playhouse stood firm; all the children were rattled, but they were safe. I thank the Lord for the small voice I heard warning me to rebuild.

Scripture tells us that the New Jerusalem has not one foundation, but twelve. The number 12 is prominent in the Bible. From Revelation 21:10-27 we see 12 gates, 12 pearls, 12 angels, 12 foundations, and we will see 12 kinds of fruits. I believe the very construction of the New Jerusalem ties together the Old and New Testaments. Since names are written on them, we can see that the 12 foundations represent the 12 Apostles and the 12 gates represent the 12 tribes of Israel. In ancient days the pearl was considered the most highly valued of all the precious stones. A pearl is formed through the oyster's pain which very well may symbolize Christ's suffering. Besides, it speaks to the eternal beauty that can come from temporary suffering.

The final observation about New Jerusalem comes from the last Chapter in the Bible. It is written by John the Revelator:

"Then the angel showed me the river of the water of life, as clear as crystal, flowing from the throne of God and of the Lamb down the middle of the great street of the city. On each side of the river stood the tree of life, bearing twelve crops of fruit, yielding its fruit every month. And the leaves of the tree are for the healing of the nations. No longer will there be any curse. The throne of God and of the Lamb will be in the city, and his servants will serve him. They will see his face, and his name will be on their foreheads. There will be no more night. They will not need the light of a lamp or the light of the sun, for the Lord God will give them light. And they will reign for ever and ever" (Revelation 22:1-5).

We have a clear message and promise that God will take care of His people's need for water, food and physical well-being. Original readers of this text lived in dry climates that demanded drawing water from guarded wells and springs. This water would have sediments in it that contributed to poor health. The water flowing from the river of life is fresh, pure and uncontaminated, able to satisfy the deepest thirst. Beyond satisfying physical thirst, this water signifies the deep fulfillment of our spiritual needs as well.

As we know, rivers flow to the sea, and there is no exception for the river of life. This is another reason why I believe there indeed will be seas on the New Earth. The prophet Ezekiel showed us a picture of where this river ends.

"He asked me, 'Son of man, do you see this?' Then he led me back to the bank of the river. When I arrived there, I saw a great number of trees on each side of the river. He said to me, 'This water flows toward the eastern region and goes down into the Arabah, where it enters the Dead Sea. When it empties into the sea, the salty water there becomes fresh. Swarms of living creatures will live wherever the river flows. There will be large numbers of fish because this water flows there and makes the salt water fresh; so where the river flows everything will live. Fishermen will stand along the shore; from En Gedi to En Eglaim there will be places for spreading nets. The fish will be of many kinds—like the fish of the Mediterranean Sea.'" (Ezekiel 47:6-11).

There are between 700,000 to 1,000,000 species of animals[26] living in the ocean (seas). Since everything will be made new, it is hard to imagine God abandoning these creatures He created.

On the banks of this river access to the tree of life is forever restored (see Revelation 2:7). At the second coming of Christ, there is no mention of the tree of the knowledge of good and evil. By this time in history, man will have learned his lesson, and since only those who believe in Jesus will be allowed in, the issue of allegiance, obedience, and devotion will already have been established. There will be no more prohibitions in Heaven.

The Greek word to describe the healing for the nations that comes from the leaves of the tree is *therapiah* (see Revelation 22:2). We get our word therapeutic from it. It's not that the nations would be diseased, but rather these leaves would be health-giving. Again, God is communicating that we will live happy, healthy and secure lives.

In Heaven we will rule with Christ; our dominion is rewarded to us through our service here. John tells us, "You have made them (people from every tribe, language, and people) to be a kingdom and priests to serve our God, and they will reign on the earth" (Revelation 5:10).

The model of reigning on the New Earth, "the government" in Heaven will not be a democracy, a republic, communism or socialism. Instead, it will be a monarchy, ruled by a benevolent King; Jesus Christ. Every citizen of Heaven will have an appointed role, one that fulfills him or her and contributes to the whole. We will be equipped to rule, and even now God is grooming us for leadership and responsibilities. Our service will bring glory to God and joy to us. Yet, regardless of your level of responsibility in Heaven, no one will feel worthless or insignificant, just as no one will feel arrogant. While there will be an administrative hierarchy, there will not be a social or relational hierarchy. There will be no pride, envy, back-stabbing or anything else sin-related.

When we consider the immensity, beauty, wealth, and presence of God in the New Jerusalem on the New Earth, merged with the New Heaven our minds quickly reach the limits of imagination. And while we cannot fully conceive what God has prepared for those who love Him, we do have the insight of what the Holy Spirit has revealed to us in this text (see 1 Corinthians 2:9-10).

I have spent much of my life thinking about the "good old days," with a longing in my heart to return to a more youthful me. Now that my life is more than half over, and as a result of this study on the life beyond, I find myself projecting ahead. If even a few years older, how grand it would be. I would be all that much closer to my forever home. My choice for Heaven and my choice for Jesus have been made. Now it is your turn.

I hope to see you there!

CHAPTER 13 - FROM DEATH TO LIFE

"People say all the time 'I don't have a good testimony'
because they think their story has to involve some
dramatic story of change from 'bad' to 'good.' But Jesus
didn't come to save people this way. Sin doesn't make us
bad it makes us dead. Jesus came to save by bringing the
dead to life. And that's an amazing testimony."

Louie Giglio

Along with my two brothers and four sisters, I was raised in a very religious family. Regular church attendance, as well as enrollment in church-sponsored schools from 1st through 12th grade, established a spiritual foundation in my life. I never questioned the existence of God, the deity of Jesus Christ, His virgin birth, Jesus' death, burial and resurrection, His ascension into Heaven and the triune nature of God. My knowledge of God was above average, and my religious disciplines of prayer, service and church attendance were respectable. Having received infant baptism, I felt secure in my future with God. I am thankful for my upbringing and my parents.

In my youth, I believed my salvation was based on my commitment to God and to church. I could not say I had a personal relationship with Jesus. I never declared Jesus to be my Savior or my Lord, and I thought that my passage into Heaven would be based on my Christian merit. I used this pedigree as a cover up for behavior that was anything but godly. Honestly, my heart was far from God.

My father was a schoolteacher while my mother remained at home, providing for her large family. Their faith gave me the security that they would never divorce, along with the genuine feeling that they loved me.

I remember their household income forced them to be on a tight budget; at least compared to all my friends. God provided the money needed to satisfy our needs, but never enough it seemed to meet our wants. My parents had their hands full raising seven children, paying the mortgage and keeping food on the table. And in my opinion, this contributed to a level of stress that I did not want to replicate in my adulthood.

As I entered High School, I made up my mind that when I became an adult, I would find peace and contentment at whatever the cost. I questioned my faith and assumed peace and happiness could only be found through the material realm with an abundance of wealth.

So, at age 14, I set a goal to be content in life and to do this I would need to earn lots of money. To produce a substantial income, I reasoned I would need a good education. To get a good college education, I would strive to receive a college scholarship, for I did not want to burden my parents with helping me come up with the needed tuition.

With this goal established, halfway through my freshman year in high school, I applied myself to academics and overachieved my way to becoming a straight A student. Working beyond my natural capabilities proved to be very stressful, so I looked for outlets to relieve the pressure. I tried athletics, which I enjoyed but was never much good at it. I tried adrenaline by getting involved in amateur motorcycle racing, which again I enjoyed but never excelled. Somewhere along the way, I developed the attitude of "work hard – play hard."

Outside of school, I began to give my energy to girls, to drugs and alcohol, and to parties. My fellow scholars, like my fellow partying friends, had little idea of my Jekyll and Hyde personality and how my moral character was remarkably different from one situation to the next. I became extraordinarily self-centered and yet, because of my childhood faith, was under the false assumption that I was living a life pleasing to God.

I received a four-year college scholarship and earned a Bachelor of Science Degree in Electrical Engineering Technology. Along the way, however, I gave up on the church. When I was 16 years old, a friend and I worked at my former grade school on Wednesday nights as janitors to clean up the gym after a weekly fund-raising event. The two families who organized this fundraiser were highly admired in the church and, I'm sure, generated lots of money through their efforts. The husbands typically arrived early to set things up and then left their wives in charge after they went home. These women were bad influences, as they contributed to my delinquency.

They taught us how to siphon gasoline from cars so that we could fill up their gas tanks. In return, they offered us beer and booze. They talked us into "streaking" (running naked through the hall wearing boxers on our heads). I did not participate in running for, if I were caught, my dad would have been hugely disappointed, so I talked a few of my friends into doing this; all in exchange for a case of Coors beer. These housewives next offered us a bottle of Jack Daniels Whiskey to perform a strip-tease act in their presence. Again, I arranged a friend to do this as I watched from the sidelines.

At first, I thought the weekly source of free alcohol was like hitting the jackpot. Every night, by quitting time, these women were drunk and showed me a side of adulthood I did not know existed. Over time, seeing them at church on Sunday mornings, I became disgusted at the dualism I saw. Based on my observations, coupled with the fact that religion did not seem to help me find peace, I walked away from the church.

I went through college leading my class academically. I also developed the habit of smoking pot almost daily, drinking heavily on the weekends, and occasionally using whatever high-end drugs I could get my hands on. I had a part-time job working in a pizza parlor that introduced me to girls who were looking for love and willingly offered sex in exchange.

As a senior in college, my partying caught up with me. Totally drunk, I jumped on my motorcycle and shortly after collided headfirst into a pickup truck. I ended up shattering my right leg. I remember signing the authorization for the doctor to amputate. Only by the grace of God was my leg saved. Until I underwent an ankle joint replacement surgery, this injury changed my athletic pursuits and became a thorn in my side.

Upon graduation, I was given a fantastic job of earning twice my father's income in my first year of employment. I also married my wife (40 years later we are still married), bought our first house, a couple of new cars, and my wife and I had our first child. My goal of making money came true. I was involved in the emerging high-technology sector at the right time. Pay increases were regular, and stock options were standard. I had made it.

However, by age 30, I faced that stark reality that I was as stressed out as my parents had ever been; and I was only raising one child, not seven! The goal of finding peace not only eluded me but also baffled me. I tried religion, athletics, academics, sex, drugs, rock-n-roll, alcohol, and materialism. Additionally, I enjoyed the esteem of being a highly paid professional with over 100 subordinates, but my life was empty and frustrating. I was dead in my sins!

I found myself disillusioned with no clue about the meaning and purpose of my life. I remember writing my wife a letter informing her that I was going to leave her and my daughter, to go to Oregon with the hopes of finding a commune to live in. I waited to hand her that letter until the timing was right. God had other plans.

At my job, I had advanced to the status of an Operations Manager. Our production facility handled over 4,000 unique parts in the manufacture of computer peripherals. How these parts were inventoried was a complicated process, prone to human error.

We hired an Industrial Engineer reporting to me who was assigned the project of automating the inventorying of parts by utilizing a bar-code scanning system. The person we hired, my age, was brilliant, and perhaps, the most content human being I had ever met to that point. His peace and joyful attitude were exactly what I had been searching for my entire life. I had to find out his secret and was dismayed when he told me it was his relationship with Jesus. I didn't understand what he was saying, all I knew of religion was rule-based, not relationship-based. I stubbornly declined to listen to what he wanted to share with me. Meanwhile, I hung onto the letter I had written to my wife.

My new friend did not let go of me, however. He saw the emptiness of my soul along with the desperation of my search. Though I was his boss, he was respectful and knew the limits of how hard and how often he could bring the subject of Biblical faith into our conversations. He knew the power of prayer and had his home Bible Study group regularly praying for me. Over time, I realized that he was not going to stop trying to reach me, so I challenged him that if he could prove even one thing to be true in the Bible, then I would read it. I felt like faith, and Biblical truth could only be blindly accepted and not proven. I was proven wrong.

As the bar-coding project gained momentum, my friend's performance began to drop dramatically. He started arriving late to work and applied himself half-heartedly to his duties. I was contemplating firing him. Then he revealed his source of inner struggle.

The UPC (Universal Product Code) system he was implementing used three guard bars or timing marks. These timing marks are a set of three 6's. This meant that my friend was tasked with putting the number 666, or the "mark of the beast" (a stamped image or seal of the Antichrist), all over our factory. He felt like he was doing the work of the devil.

Having watched a popular mystic/cult movie called The Omen, I was fully aware of the meaning of 666. My interest was piqued when he told me that, in the Bible, there is a reference to the mark of the beast. It stated that this mark would impact global economics. One day, in my office, he opened his Bible and had me read the following passage:

"It (Satan) also forced all people, great and small, rich and poor, free and slave, to receive a mark on their right hands or on their foreheads, so that they could not buy or sell unless they had the mark, which is the name of the beast or the number of its name. This calls for wisdom. Let the person who has insight calculate the number of the beast, for it is the number of a man. That number is 666" (Revelation 13:16-18).

In my mind, he had just proved to me something true from in the Bible. This shared information sealed my interest, enough to begin reading the Bible for myself.

Six years earlier, when we married, a religious aunt, asked my mom what she should buy us for a gift. As my mom relayed the question to me, I rather flippantly suggested that she send us a Bible. After our honeymoon, we received a large, red, Bible – complete with pictures. We opened it, put it back into the box it came in and stored it away. My wife and I forgot all about it.

The day my friend had me read the Revelation passage in the Bible, I asked my wife where our Bible was located. She thought I was nuts. She had no recollection of what I was talking about. I ended up going through every box of storage we had in our house. There, in the back of a closet, I found the Bible, along with a few other forgotten wedding gifts.

My nightly routine after work was to change from my dress clothes into a comfortable pair of blue jeans and a T-shirt, light up a marijuana joint, and down a few beers. I would cap this off with a bourbon and water over ice. My Jekyll and Hyde days stuck with me. The first day I read the Bible was no different. I went through my routine, and once I was comfortably high, I read Revelation, Chapter 13. Then I went on to read all of Revelation. What a trip!

The next evening, I repeated my actions. Dope, beer, bourbon, and the Bible. Again, I was captivated by what I read. I began to repeat this pattern every day until one day I decided to read the Gospels. There I rediscovered the stories told that I had heard in church as a kid. I had always wondered where they were in the Bible; now I knew.

Getting high and reading the Bible was beginning to dominate my daily routine. I was starting to think I must have recently bought some good pot. I then decided to read the Bible sober-minded to see if the impact would be the same.

Amazingly, I was even more captivated and soon began reading the Bible for up to 2 hours every night. My wife thought I was just going through another of my self-centered phases. In truth, the Word of God was breaking through my hardened heart.

One day, as I stood at my kitchen sink doing the dishes and looking out over the empty field next to our house, I was struck as though by lightning with the reality that Jesus is God; that He loves me and that He died on the cross for all my sins. In an instant, without attending church and without saying a prayer, I was changed from the inside out – I was a new man. I was alive!

Just like the thief on the cross, I received mercy and grace. I had yet to lift a finger to prove my worthiness, but I didn't have to. I was saved, born again, and declared righteous before God based on His merits, not mine. My love for the Word of God stems from knowing that, "All Scripture is God-breathed and is useful for teaching, rebuking, correcting and training in righteousness, so that the servant of God may be thoroughly equipped for every good work" (2 Timothy 3:16-17).

Who would imagine that the evangelistic verse which initially captured my heart would be the one found in Revelation concerning the mark of the beast? The Word of God is active and alive, sharper than any double-edged sword (see Hebrews 4:12).

There in my kitchen, following my encounter with the living God, I immediately emptied my liquor cabinet and poured hundreds of dollars of booze down the drain. No longer did I need alcohol to usher in a false sense of peace. Giving up pot took me a little longer, but the cocaine and other drugs ended promptly.

One year later, after observing the changes God made in me, my wife also accepted Jesus as her Lord and Savior. We began faithfully attending a Bible-based church. Seven years later I was hired on staff at that church. The letter I had written about leaving my wife, was never delivered and it has since been lost.

Today I am blessed beyond measure with three adult children and their fantastic spouses. We have four adorable grandchildren. Beyond all, I rejoice in knowing my destination is certain. I have possession of peace and contentment that comes from my Heavenly Father. This is the same peace offered to all humankind. As you read this book may your heart and mind be filled with the knowledge of God and may you too allow Him to write, or add to, your conversion story.

ENDNOTES

1 https://thevisualcommunicationguy.com/2014/05/19/the-worlds-18-most-widely-read-books/

2 https://christianity.stackexchange.com/questions/8490/into-how-many-languages-has-the-bible-been-translated

3 https://happyscience-na.org/about/teachings/happy-science-and-buddhism/eternal-life-and-reincarnation/

4 https://www.urbandictionary.com/define.php?term=nirvana

5 Catechism of the Catholic Church, 1994, United States Catholic Conference, Liberia Editrice Vaticana, pp 268-269.

6 Apocrypha, 2 Maccabees, 12:38-46

7 https://www.washingtonpost.com/news/morning-mix/wp/2018/04/11/the-boy-who-came-back-from-heaven-now-wants-his-day-in-court/?utm_term=.5004974d3e23

8 https://en.wikipedia.org/wiki/The_Boy_Who_Came_Back_from_Heaven

9 Romans 6:23, Ephesians 2:8-9

10 Romans 10:9-13

11 Romans 10:13

12 John 1:12

13 John 5:24

14 2 Thessalonians 1:8-9

15 http://time.com/3915168/solitary-confinement/

16 "Evidence that Demands a Verdict" by Josh McDowell and "The Case for Christ" by Lee Strobel.

17 https://courses.lumenlearning.com/sociology/chapter/social-constructions-of-reality/

18 1 Samuel 18:6-16, 1 Samuel 19:1-11

19 1 Samuel 20:1-13

20 https://www.christianitytoday.com/history/issues/issue-25/life-times-of-d-l-moody.html

21 Restored, Easter 2017, Cornerstone Church, Iowa

22 http://www.bible-researcher.com/canon1.html

23 https://todayinsci.com/A/Asimov_Isaac/AsimovIsaac-Fear-Quotations.htm

[24] Genesis 1:3,10,12,18,21,25
[25] https://bigthink.com/paul-ratner/how-many-people-have-ever-lived-on-planet-earth
[26] https://www.seeker.com/two-thirds-marine-species-remain-unknown-1766300637.html

BIBLIOGRAPHY

Alcorn, Randy. Heaven. Nashville, Tennessee: Tyndale House Publishers, 2004.

Baxter, J. Sidlow. *The Other Side of Death*. Grand Rapids, Michigan: Kregel, 1987.

Easton's Bible Dictionary. New York City, New York. Scripture Press, 1893.

Eldredge, John. *All Things New*. Nashville, Tennessee: Thomas Nelson, 2017.

Strobel, Lee. *The Case For Christ*. Grand Rapids, Michigan: Zondervan; Updated, Expanded edition, (September 6, 2016).

McDowell, Josh. *Evidence That Demands a Verdict*. Nashville, Tennessee: Thomas Nelson, 1992.

Trousdale, Jerry. *Miraculous Movements: How Hundreds of Thousands of Muslims Are Falling in Love with Jesus*. Nashville, Tennessee: Thomas Nelson, 2012.

Youngblood, Ronald. *Nelson's Bible Dictionary*. Nashville, Tennessee: Thomas Nelson, 1986.

Made in the USA
Monee, IL
07 February 2023

27304312R00100